MURDER & MAYHEM
—— IN THE ——
FINGER LAKES

MURDER & MAYHEM
— IN THE —
FINGER LAKES

R. MARCIN

THE
History
PRESS

Published by The History Press
Charleston, SC
www.historypress.com

First published 2020

Manufactured in the United States

ISBN 9781467146142

Library of Congress Control Number: 2020938617

CONTENTS

.

A NOTE ON THE SOURCES

Their absence of psychosocial insight notwithstanding, newspapers of the nineteenth and early twentieth centuries are unsurpassed in their vivid depictions of the era and the lives of its inhabitants. They nonetheless demonstrate an understanding of human nature sufficient to cover murder trials voluminously, delivering cinematically detailed scenes to those denied the privilege of witnessing the proceedings. In unrestrained prose, they offer fragmented portraits of individuals plagued by alcoholism, domestic violence, poverty and illnesses both physical and mental. Editorials, functioning as a Greek chorus, illuminate the degree of sympathy these transgressors aroused and the zeitgeist surrounding them.

Whether the perpetrators disappeared from history or had paragraphs devoted to their final moments, their stories captivated the public. They provided a diversion so desperately needed that people would walk all night to view or be near the site of their executions; they also stirred elemental fears of a disrupted social order. Motives are eternally familiar—jealousy, covetousness, an injured ego—or obscure even to themselves. Regardless of how far they may be from us, historically or psychologically, the perpetrators and their victims remain embodiments of the unexpected turns any life can take.

Chapter 1
GEORGE CHAPMAN

Waterloo, Seneca County
1828

At a time specified only as after the Sullivan-Clinton campaign of 1779, a road was planked from Geneva to the outlet of Seneca Lake. Concurrent with this occasion, an Englishman, James "Uncle Jimmy" Nares, erected a brick-and-concrete tavern on the south side of the road above the lake, over the Seneca County border. From his fondness of field sports and foxhunting originated the name Sportsman's Hall for the new public house, and its doors were "open to all lovers of fun and frolic."[1]

On Sunday, July 20, 1828, all future associations of "fun" with Nares's establishment came to an end, courtesy of an encounter between his fellow countryman George Chapman, a tailor, and Daniel Wright, a mixed-race hostler at the hall. The origin of their conflict is obscure, but the earliest report, in the *Geneva Gazette* of July 23, claimed that they had a quarrel and happened to meet about the middle of the day at Nares's. They "talked it over" and were reconciled, but "according to a vulgar custom," they had to "satisfy their treaty of amity over a bottle of whiskey."

Sixty years after the incident, the *Geneva Advertiser* gave the most specific account. The men at work on the canal, occupying the temporary shanties in the neighborhood of Sportsman's Hall, made nightly raids on the Nareses' currant bushes, especially on Sunday. Mrs. Nares, fearing she would be stripped of her entire crop, requested Wright to "endeavor to prevent the pilfering." Wright allegedly found Chapman in the garden picking and eating currants, and "the first ill-feeling" arose from his remonstrance with the plunderer. This was soon smoothed over, before they drank heavily together and became intoxicated. In the words of the *Geneva Gazette*, "here the smothered flame of resentment again burst forth."

While in the garden attached to the premises, the pair engaged in a scuffle, and Wright apparently threw Chapman. After this, they separated for a while, and Chapman vowed he would "kill the d----d negro," "using very threatening and violent language."[2] Wright went into the granary and lay on an oat bin, either to escape danger or to go to sleep. Some time afterward, Chapman sought him, shook him awake and said, "I am going to kill you." Wright, still befogged by alcohol, replied, "If you must kill me, kill me." With both hands, Chapman seized a nearby spade and struck Wright four or five blows on the side of the head.

Chapman went into the hall, announced what he had done and was taken into custody. Wright was carried inside and died about an hour afterward. Chapman "exulted in what he had done," according to the *New York American*—"he had killed the d----d negro and was glad of it." The *Geneva Gazette*, however, reported "after the frenzy of the liquor subsided, the mind of the wretched murderer awakened to a sense of the horrid deed he had perpetrated and to the inevitable doom which awaits him." After his apprehension, Chapman said "he had been a soldier—had helped kill a good many men—and now must be hung for killing a d----d negro."

Although Chapman and Wright had originally been labeled "excessively intemperate drinkers," Chapman was later characterized as "ordinarily a quiet and good citizen," and historians unanimously agreed he was "a decent fellow when sober."[3] He had been a soldier in the British army, deserted from Canada and came to New York, where he resided on the north side of William Street in Geneva, some years before he came to public attention. Before the murder, he was employed by William Rodney, who had been the military tailor at West Point. The *New York American* pronounced Chapman's habits "very irregular." As for Wright, the sole description of his character defined him as "a very decent man" despite his addiction to liquor.

Chapman, reportedly chained to a staple in the floor of the jail in the Waterloo Courthouse, was arraigned at a circuit court of Oyer and Terminer in Waterloo on Thursday, April 16, 1829. Although the fact of murder was admitted, Chapman's counsel attempted to set up a plea of insanity, "on which point many witnesses were examined, and every effort made to sustain the defence which talent and ingenuity could suggest."[4] At 1:00 a.m. on

Postcard depicting the courthouse and county buildings at Waterloo, with the jail on the far right. *Courtesy Seneca County historian.*

Friday, the case was submitted to the jury, and between one and two hours later it pronounced the defendant guilty. With rhetoric displaying "more than ordinary talents," Judge Moseley sentenced Chapman "to expiate on the gallows the violated laws of God and man" on Thursday, May 28. The prisoner received the verdict with little apparent emotion and throughout the trial had given "the appearance of a firmness and resolution which he could not have possessed."[5]

In an outré journalistic twist, the newspapers offered no pontifications on the justice of the sentence but rather spied an opening to preach the virtues of temperance and piety. The *Waterloo Observer*, in torrid, creatively spelled prose, pointed to Chapman as a personification of the misfortunes spawned by dipsomania:

> *The trial presented a case of the most cold blooded murder, and yet so artless, that charity and vengeance almost combated for the influence of the mind. The only defence set up by the prisoner's counsel was that of insanity—and to this point of the case the attention of every man, who abberates from that state of sobriety, and that uninflamed exercise of reason with which the God of nature has blessed him, should seriously be called. George Chapman was a few years since a* sober man, *and had he continued so, he might have been a useful mechanic and respected citizen; but alas! the accursed BOTTLE—that to which the Gallows, and State Prison, and the Lunatic Asylum, and poverty, and disease, and death, are more indebted for their subjects than to all other causes combined—lured him to its embrace, and with its usual discipline of innulcating idleness, withdrawing character, stifling shame, and rendering the heart callous, has now brought him to the verge of an ignominious death. Well did Judge*

Moseley in his remarks prefixing the sentence of the law, call the attention of the numerous audience which had assembled on that occasion, to this besetting sin of the day, and beseech them, that as they now could appreciate the legitimate consequences of this evil, they would themselves abandon, if in the least degree embraced, and encourage the abandonment in others, of this most prevalent and most pernicious vice.

Intoxication was the sole cause of this murder. There was no deadly revenge to gratify—no pecuniary consideration to induce—nothing, which in the view of a sober man, could be considered as the least possible object. It in fact resulted from the dictates of the spirit of—RUM.

The *Geneva Gazette* of May 21 believed that the parties' intoxication was "rather an aggravation than an extenuation of the crime":

Had they been discharging the duties of religion, which are equally binding upon all; had they been in the Sunday School (neither of them, we are informed, could read or write;) instead of a violent or ignominious death, they might now have been useful citizens—living the life and preparing to "die the death of the righteous," and their "latter end" would "be like his."

But their race is run. All that remains is to hold them up as warnings to others: and shall they be in vain? Will the youth of this village remember their Creator in the days of their youth—improve their opportunities to gain knowledge—keep the Sabbath day holy—respect their superiors—dash the poisoned bowl from their lips, and flee from every vice?

From the time of his sentence, Chapman allegedly refused to eat and repeatedly declared his intention to starve himself. On May 13, he was "extremely low, and it is doubtful he lives till the appointed day." The *Gazette* believed "it is likely this determination would have been carried into effect" but for the "kind and judicious management of the Sheriff."

Such an outcome would have been a disappointment to a considerable segment of the populace, for perhaps the largest gathering ever held in the region for decades to come was at Waterloo on the day of the execution. The dismayed *Gazette* testified:

On this occasion that strange and mortifying propensity of our species which seems to delight in the misery and suffering of our fellow beings, was indulged to its fullest extent. Although at a season of the year when merchants, mechanics, and particularly farmers, are unusually engaged, and the weather oppressively warm, there was what may emphatically be termed a general "turn out." Though at the distance of six miles from the place of execution, our streets, between the hours of six and ten in the morning, were literally crowded with wagons and horses, bearing the curious and we may add thoughtless multitude to witness one of the most awful spectacles the imagination can conceive. Several thousands of persons, and many of them from a great distance, passed thro' this village on the morning of the execution.

A more jocular letter to the editor, printed in the *Geneva Advertiser* in November 1894, provided an account from an "aged informant":

With many others he went down to Waterloo on a canal boat. The boat was gaily decked out for the occasion, with music, and banners floating in the breeze, girls and their lovers dressed in their best, all "going to see a man hanged." There's no accounting for taste! Some parties—one at least that he knows of positively—took this canal boat ride as a wedding trip.... The trees about the grounds were fairly black with men and boys, all anxious to see the sight. Booths and stalls could be seen in all directions, whose owners were bartering their wares. You will never get an old Seneca County man to admit that Waterloo has ever before or since seen so large a crowd as on the day Chagman [sic] was hung...I speak of the canal boat crowd. It was nothing compared to the hundreds of wagon loads, and the many hundreds who went to Waterloo on foot from all directions, some actually walking twenty miles.

All night, one heard the tramp of feet, horses' hooves and the wheels of vehicles from the east crossing the Cayuga Lake bridge. According to a letter published in the *Advertiser* on February 10, 1855, many people came from as far away as Pennsylvania. "They came in ox-carts, four horse teams, by boat and packet, and many slept out-of-doors as there were no accommodations for so many visitors," claimed the *Ovid Gazette* on the centennial of the execution. The stream of humanity trudging toward Waterloo proceeded for hours without interruption. A man who walked from Ithaca was so fatigued that he fell asleep and "failed to see the ghastly sight."[6] Gratis DeYoe, who witnessed the execution from a tree, said that the crowd packed every avenue and covered the roofs of buildings. As a correspondent of the *Geneva Gazette* expressed it in 1887, "It was as big a day as a 'general trainin'."

The crowd at Waterloo was estimated between ten and fifteen thousand. The *Gazette* believed the actual number might have been much larger than the highest estimate.

At about 12:30 p.m. on May 28, the military drew up in front of the jail, and within minutes Chapman was taken from his cell. In the company of Sheriff James Rorison, the district attorney and clergymen, he was escorted down the street later known as Locust to the place of execution, West Island (now Oak Island) in the Seneca outlet, in the village of Waterloo. The Fayette rifles and a brass band headed the solemn procession, the band playing "The Rogue's March."

Chapman was dressed in a flowing white robe, white cap, white stockings and "thin shoes." "His countenance was pale and haggard in the extreme, and his whole frame trembled. His whole appearance bespoke the utmost wretchedness and despair."[7]

Nearly half an hour later, Chapman ascended the scaffold unassisted "and with great apparent firmness." Reverend Aaron Lane of Waterloo addressed the assemblage "in appropriate, solemn and impressive language. He directed their attention to the awful and admonitory spectacle before them, and adverted to the cause which had led to this heart-rending and melancholy exhibition, and which was the general cause of the similar exhibitions which so frequently disgrace our land, to wit, the ruinous and guilty practice of *intemperance.*"[8]

The ceremonies complete, Chapman spoke with several people on the scaffold and then stepped onto the drop, "apparently for the purpose of viewing its construction and of determining the length of rope he should

Aerial view of Oak Island. *Courtesy Seneca County historian.*

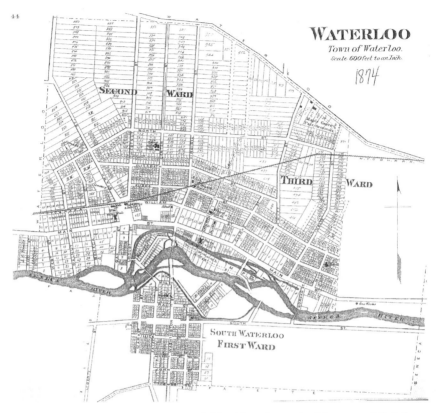

WATERLOO

Town of Waterloo.
Scale 600 feet to an Inch.

1874

Second Ward

Third Ward

South Waterloo
First Ward

1874 map of the village of Waterloo. Oak Island is to the south of Seneca and Oak Streets. *Courtesy Seneca County historian.*

fall."[9] After standing a minute, "perfectly composed and looking around the gazing and anxious crowd,"[10] he descended the platform. The sheriff loosely pinioned his arms and adjusted the rope around his neck. Chapman took a red handkerchief in his hand and returned, again with assistance, to the drop. His last words were, "Oh, God, have mercy on my poor soul and forgive me all my sins."

The sheriff fastened the rope to the beam, and Chapman, the cap drawn over his eyes, threw the handkerchief. Before it reached the ground, the drop was released, and within three minutes, Chapman was dead.

The crowd's reaction to this does not appear in contemporary sources, but it may be surmised from the *Geneva Gazette*'s closing paragraph in its account:

> *From what we witnessed on this occasion we are confirmed in our belief, that public executions are any thing but salutary; and that the punishment*

pronounced against the highest offence known to our law loses much of its terror from the circumstances of pomp and parade under which it is inflicted. There was nothing of that solemnity and awe which the occasion should have excited. The careless jest, the vociferous laugh, and sounds of merriment and festivity, were heard mingling with the solemn note of preparation which was to send a fellow being to the retributions of eternity. We trust that the arm of the law will shortly be interposed, to prevent the repetition of such exhibitions.

With a century's worth of embellishments allowed to proliferate, and no eyewitnesses left to offer a contradiction, the veracity of this statement from the *Geneva Daily Times* may be accepted at one's own risk: "The great mass of people were satisfied like the ancient Romans after a Christian martyr had been fed to the lions and when the body of the little tailor was cut down and taken away by his sisters, broken hearted as they were they were glowered at by the gaping mass who had their holiday and had feasted on the spectacle."[11]

Chapman's body was brought to Geneva by boat and buried in a ten-acre lot "on the west side of the Lyons road some distance north of North Street."[12] It was rumored that the doctors were eager to obtain the body for dissection, so a night watch was set. One night, upon a false alarm, Adam Wilson fired his overloaded gun, which burst, shooting off one of his fingers and shattering his hand. Rumors circulated that the body had been taken up and buried elsewhere, sunk in the lake or sold to the college, "but it is not known whether those in the secret ever divulged the actual facts."[13] After two weeks, noted the *Advertiser*, no one seemed to care much.

According to another anonymous recollection, the excitement attending the execution "was nothing compared with the events following immediately after."[14] "In those days whiskey was only about 30 cents a gallon, and when a man wanted to celebrate he did not think of buying less than a quarter, and what he could not drink he gave away, so that a good many men could get drunk on ten cents." That is exactly what the Geneva crowd did at Waterloo, including six or eight Englishmen and as many Irishmen. They returned home en masse, probably by boat. "After talking a little while, some Irishmen would sing out, 'Well, they hanged the d----d Englishman at last,' and the English coats would come off and there would be a scrap. Then when affairs grew too quiet, an Englishman would rejoin, 'They hanged the blasted Irishman,' and then Erins' coats would be peeled and another scrap followed. Old Jimmy Earl boasted afterwards that he was in eleven fights on that day on the way home."[15]

On January 9, 1887, inmate Charles Johnson murdered turnkey John Walters during an attempted jailbreak at Waterloo. His subsequent trial and execution on November 15, 1888, prompted a number of reminiscences from those present at the last execution in Seneca County. The *Rochester Democrat* noted that the room in which Chapman was sentenced "is shown by the 'old inhabitants' to those who are curious minded." An unsigned response in the *Geneva Gazette* claimed, "Though but seven years old at the time we distinctly remember being taken to see the body of the murdered man as it was prepared for burial….The murderous weapon as it glanced from the negro's forehead made two distinct indentations in the lid of the oat-bin, which with the streams of blood as it trickled across the lid and down the inside of the bin were visible for many years."[16]

The *Geneva Advertiser* may have been speaking for many when it announced it had heard the story of the murder "a score of times at the family hearth, and since at the meetings of the Historical Society." As the time of Chapman's execution drew near, "the wildest excitement pervaded the country for many miles around, and preparations were made on all sides by the making of new clothes and garments to wear at the hanging, just as if the people were going to attend a great fete."[17] It was even reported that Chapman made a suit for Sheriff Rorison, who wore it to the execution. When thousands gathered at Waterloo in 1879 to celebrate the Sullivan centennial, many aged people remarked that no such multitude of people had been seen since Chapman was hanged.

A Mr. Lettic, who worked for the Seneca County historian, often repeated a story, passed down by his father, a witness to the hanging. As Chapman walked between the sheriff and his spiritual adviser, a man trailing along asked Chapman if he could assist him. "No," said the condemned man, "you owe me for a suit of clothes that I made for you and I want no assistance from such as you."

Although its popularity waned after Chapman's execution and Sportsman's Hall stood vacant for years, history repeated itself in 1911. On August 31, the *Geneva Gazette* reported that one man was dead and another at jail in Waterloo awaiting the coroner's verdict "as the result of a barroom jangle" at the tavern, which had been the subject of strange stories. Marvin Clarke spoke of the size of his glass of beer, "words followed, and young Nicholas Sauerborn struck him and ordered him out. He went out, fell to the ground and died. An autopsy shows no indication that a blow heavy enough to kill was struck. The man probably was scared to death."

Chapter 2

JOHN FITZGERALD

Sterling, Cayuga County
1855

Even after verbal outbursts of homicidal rage reached a climax, the dynamics of the Fitzgerald family remained concealed from the public. A cruel, abusive and oppressive relationship may have existed; perhaps the expressions of smoldering enmity stemmed from persecutory delusions. In the absence of insight into the perpetrator's motives, the citizens of Cayuga County—barely recovered from the shocks delivered by the crimes of Henry Wyatt, William Freeman and the Baham brothers—were left reeling from another demonstration of human depravity, not from a madman but rather an apparent monster, one responsible for "a deed which exceeds in enormity the Van Ness [*sic*] murder as far as did that all the known similar crimes that had preceded it."[18]

In May 1855, the Fitzgerald household consisted of Mark, a day laborer and owner of a small farm, and his wife, Mary, as well as their sons Patrick, twenty-one; John, eighteen; and James, thirteen. In 1846, they had settled about five miles north of Sterling Center, in a one-and-a-half-story frame house at the end of a remote road. A partition divided the house into two rooms—a kitchen with a recess and what was known as the square room. Mark and Mary slept in the kitchen in the winter and the square room in the summer; when the older boys were not away working, Pat generally slept with James in the recess, while John occupied the square room.

In June, John asked a family acquaintance, William Cooper of Sterling, if he had heard the fuss they had at their house when his brother Barney died. Yes, Cooper had heard something about it; he told John he thought it best for him "to keep cool and not appear so hard towards his people as he did."[19] John said if he had a gun the day Barney was buried, he would have shot the cross and the old man too—meaning his father, whom he usually called "the old man" or "old Fitz." Cooper told John that he was disgracing himself more than his father in talking so about his people. "By God I will shoot the old man anyway," John retorted.

Cooper was on the receiving end of another of John's tirades about his father sometime in July, when their paths crossed in the town of Oswego. John initiated the exchange, as he had last time, saying "the old man" had forbidden George McEackron from paying him his wages and that he was going to leave the country. Cooper asked him where he was going. John didn't know, but he would "go and maul the old man like Hell before he left."

Mark, perhaps believing reinforcement was required, brought neighbor Thomas O'Keefe to John's place of employment, McEackron's farm in Oswego. O'Keefe approached John in the lot and asked what "vexed" him. John said something to the effect that his father wouldn't let him have his wages. O'Keefe told him he had better be still and be a better boy than he had been; his father didn't want to deprive him of his wages. John swore by Jesus if his father laid a straw in his way, he had as lief kill him as kill a snake.

Mark told McEackron to pay John his wages, if John would be a "good boy, and stay his time out." John remained until July 3, after McEackron paid him all but five dollars.

By the end of July, John was living and working at the home of William McFarland in Sterling. In mid-August, a conversation arose regarding a dog William Jr. had poisoned with strychnine. John inquired about the effects of the poison and how soon it would produce death. William told him if administered in the right quantity it would take fifteen minutes. John asked how much it would take to kill a man, what the poison looked like and how much it cost. It was whiter than flour, William replied, and for one shilling he could get enough to poison twenty or thirty dogs. (He did not state under oath that he had guessed at the dose required for dispatching a human.) John wanted to know where he could get some, and William informed him that most apothecaries carried it.

THE NIGHT OF WEDNESDAY, August 29, Pat, who had returned to the residence a day or two earlier after spending time in Boston, went to bed in his usual quarters. Mark and Mary retired to their bed in the square room, and James spent the night on a lounge near his parents. John, who had moved back in the day before, declined to sleep with Pat, saying it was too warm. Wearing only his shirt and pants, he spread a blanket on the kitchen floor and lay down with a pillow.

Around 3:00 a.m., Pat was awakened by a *thump*, as though a body had fallen to the floor. John, barefoot and minus his coat, entered the kitchen from the square room and said that a few "negroes" were killing their folks; they had got hold of him and tore his shirt. Pat scrambled out of bed, grabbed a pair of pants and dashed to the kitchen door, which, he noticed, was bolted from the inside. He unlocked the door and raced to the home of Lewis O'Neil, fifteen or twenty rods away.

O'Neil may not have understood the nature of the unannounced visit, for, as he recalled, they set out for the Fitzgerald house "in consequence of something that [Pat] told." By the moonlight, O'Neil discerned an axe lying on the grass near the house and heard "something like crying" from within. With Pat in the lead, they ventured inside.

O'Neil held up a candle Pat had lit and looked around. A few feet away, John wept inconsolably. O'Neil asked him what was the matter; John replied that the "negroes" had been after him too. He didn't know where they had gone, but they had hold of him and tore his sleeve.

One of the brothers told O'Neil to hurry and go into the room. He walked up to the door, in front of which was a track of blood, as if made by a bare foot. He pushed the door open and was greeted with the sight of the square room's floor covered in blood. He approached the bed, where Mark Fitzgerald lay on his back, his head turned toward the left. O'Neil placed his hand on Mark's arm, and although he was slightly warm, there was no doubt he was dead. Mary, lying turned toward Mark with her face against his and her arm over his breast, was colder to the touch. A blow from an axe had split open her neck. In the middle of the floor, James lay on his back amid the blood. His face gaped open three inches from below his left ear to his mouth. Another wound on the left side of his face extended about three inches below the eye.

From the kitchen, a voice O'Neil thought belonged to his wife told someone to look under the bed to see if the intruders were there. O'Neil found no one, but he noticed bloody finger marks on the side of the bed.

John remained in the kitchen, crying at high volume. Although O'Neil thought John was hurt, he saw no cuts or sores about him.

Pat asked O'Neil to stay in the house while he went to summon Timothy Glenn, who lived about 120 rods from the Fitzgeralds. After Glenn headed out, Pat fetched O'Keefe and then ran as fast as he could for Dr. Proudfit, the nearest physician. The doctor started for the Fitzgerald house in his sulky, leaving Pat behind.

Glenn arrived at the house alone, finding the door open and the candle extinguished. The badly frightened O'Neil had gone home, leaving only John, still crying, sitting on a chair in the kitchen. Glenn inquired what was the matter, and John told him someone was in the house. When Glenn asked where his mother and father went, John replied, "They are in the room."

Glenn lit a candle with a match John procured and peered into the square room. He noticed James and the profusion of blood but did not go inside. He stayed in the kitchen with John until O'Keefe came about half an hour later. He, too, heard John's sobs before he entered the house.

O'Keefe stepped through the partly open door and by the light on the table saw John holding a towel "or something" to his face. O'Keefe asked what was the matter, took the candle and set forth to investigate. He found James lying in the middle of the blood-soaked square room and perceived he was still alive. He went at once to the bed and laid his hand on the corpses. The hollow between them was full of "thick blood." Mary Fitzgerald, he noted, wore very little clothing.

O'Keefe turned his attention to the boy to see what he could do for him until the doctor came. James asked for water several times, and although O'Keefe gave it to him, most of it ran out of the wounds. He said once that he was cold, and O'Keefe wrapped him in a quilt and placed a pillow beneath his head. Two or three times he told O'Keefe to take him to Lewis's, and O'Keefe finally made the attempt. He put a shawl around James, who got to his feet with "very little assistance." James reached the door of the square room and seemed about to faint, so O'Keefe laid him back where he had been. He thought James "had bled all that was in him out."

Glenn had left to notify more neighbors, and O'Keefe wandered in and out of the rooms while he waited for Dr. Proudfit. John never strayed from the kitchen. O'Keefe asked John whether anyone was there except "the old folks." John repeated that there was one or more "negroes," but no one saw any sign of the alleged perpetrators.

DR. PROUDFIT APPEARED AROUND 6:00 a.m. and immediately investigated the square room. James, covered with a quilt, lay on the floor with his head on a pillow. O'Keefe stooped over the delirious boy and held his head while James tossed from side to side. No pulse beat at his wrist, and a tablespoon held under the wound on his cheek gathered no blood. Proudfit sewed up the boy's face and turned his attention to the bodies on the bed.

Mark Fitzgerald seemed to have died without a struggle, as his hands were folded over his breast. His eyes were mostly open and his tongue protruded. A blow across the right side of his neck went clear through the spine, nearly severing his head. Without disturbing Mary Fitzgerald, Dr. Proudfit could see three cuts on her: one on the left shoulder exposing the bone, another nearly severing the spinal column and marrow about two inches higher and slightly to the right another that had missed any vital organs.

James, his wounds sewn too late, died around 7:00 a.m., raving about his mother.

KNOWLEDGE OF THE MURDERS reached Auburn Thursday afternoon by telegraph, when Sheriff Knapp was asked to send a coroner to hold an inquest on the bodies. Before this could be accomplished, Justice of the Peace George Tilford "paid some necessary attention to the corpses,"[20] took the depositions of several witnesses and issued a warrant for John Fitzgerald's arrest.

Tilford presided over an examination at the Fitzgerald house around 4:00 p.m. "John, you are brought before me on a warrant for murder," he began, "and I want to ask you some questions relative to it. You are at liberty to answer or refuse to answer as you please." John made no reply. "John, what caused them wounds on your father and mother and brother?" John's response was not recorded, but proceedings undoubtedly elicited no further information.

Constable Lewis Irwin and Peter Adle assisted John in changing his clothes in the upper part of the house that afternoon. They found a spot of blood on the left shoulder of John's shirt and another on the wristband of the right arm, which looked as if an attempt had been made to wipe it off. The toes and side of John's right foot were also covered with blood, as was the outer side of the left foot. In John's vest pocket, Irwin found a vial, about an inch and a half long and "pretty large round" for its length, nearly filled with a white substance. Most of the bottle's label had been torn off, but a test proved its contents to be strychnine.

Dr. Plumb, with whom John had once lived, urged him to tell the truth; circumstances were strongly against him, and rather than die with a lie on his soul, he should throw himself on the mercy of the law. It may have been at this point that "the monster *admitted the crime!*" in the words of the *Auburn Daily American*, but whether this occurred before or after the examination was not revealed.

One of the county coroners, L.M. Hollister of Auburn, reached the scene of the murder around 10:00 p.m. He summoned a jury as soon as he arrived and sent for the justice and the prisoner. John refused to say a word, pro or con. After considering the evidence, the jury concluded that John Fitzgerald had killed the three victims with an axe.

A REPORTER FROM THE *Auburn Weekly American* accompanied Hollister "on his dreadful errand" and the next day gave readers "particulars of a deed of fiendish murder that makes our blood run cold," one that "far exceeds in unmitigated atrocity" the murder of the Van Nest family, the standard by which all crimes were estimated.

The *Weekly American* representative left Oswego in a wagon and drove the nine miles to Sterling. Within four or five miles of the Fitzgerald residence, "we found the road filled with people, riding and on foot, going to or coming from that place." From the main road near Churchill's, about seven miles from Oswego, "we turned into a lonely and not much frequented crossroad, leading off among the hills, and into portions of the country that were but sparsely settled. But the farther we went in this direction, the more dense became the crowd, and at last our way was almost blocked up with people."

There was no mistaking the location of the murder house: vehicles of all kinds had drawn up near it, and "lights were flitting from the windows." Despite the number of people milling about, there was no noise. "Men spoke almost under their breath, and all seemed to be impressed with the overwhelming fact, that within the walls of that house were to be found proofs of one of the most horrible crimes that ever startled a civilized community."

Entering the house, the reporter was shown to the square room, where the bodies lay beneath a sheet. His description of the scene left the readers to exercise their imaginations: "The spectacle was a horrible one!" Scarcely more words were at his disposal to describe the victims: Mark Fitzgerald was "an Irishman, about 45 years of age, and some five feet nine inches high, of somewhat spare but muscular build, and with light hair, scarcely covering a rather high forehead." Mary was about fifty-two years old, "stout and fair— and evidently a woman who had led a busy life." James was summarized as "a plump and stout lad of about 15 [*sic*] years of age."

As for John, he was "a stoutly built young man" whose features "are not strongly marked by intelligence, but his expression is ordinarily smart and shrewd. His forehead is low, his hair is black, and curls a good deal. His *general* expression of countenance last night and this morning was churlish, dogged and fiendish, and yet occasionally he cried out, wringing his hands— 'Oh my poor mother! Oh my parents!!'"

Constable Irwin and Luther Longley brought John to the jail at Auburn late Saturday afternoon, September 1. The prisoner told them that if they would come to the jail the next morning, he would tell them all about it. Longley replied if Pat was innocent it was his duty to let it be known.

According to the *Weekly American*, the delay in bringing John to Auburn was caused by the Friday morning arrest of Pat and "a young woman whom Patrick and John had both paid their addresses to, and were at variance about."[21] An examination resulted in their discharge. "Indeed, John confesses that he alone did the dreadful deed, and that he *meant also to murder Patrick, and then set fire to the house!*" To this admission, the *Weekly American* could only repeat the refrain, "There is no parallel to the horrible atrocity of this treble murder."

No fewer than 1,500 people visited the house the day of the murder. "The excitement all through the region of country bordering upon the scene of these murders was great," the *Weekly American* announced. "As the news spread, the astonishment, indignation and horror of the people rose to an unprecedented pitch….A few proposed to wreak summary vengeance upon the atrocious wretch, and hang him to the first tree; but obedience to the laws rose paramount to every other consideration, and neither the culprit nor the officers were interfered with."

As far as the *Weekly American* could tell, no valid reason was given for the "*cause* of this horrible deed of blood." None of the many stories afloat could be traced, but without question John Fitzgerald was "a wild, wayward, revengeful boy." He had begun his criminal career with petty offenses, it was said; he graduated to stealing a horse, for which he was briefly incarcerated at the Auburn jail. (According to the *Auburn Daily Advertiser*, "his extreme youth excited the sympathy of many, and he was at length liberated without undergoing a regular trial before our courts."[22]) For months, he and his parents had had sharp clashes of opinion, "*Spiritual and Temporal,*" and the night before the murder he allegedly threatened to knock his mother down with a stick because she did not get his tea ready at the moment he wished it. A little over a week before, his parents had supposedly found strychnine he had mixed with their sugar, and he had threatened to shoot his father a week before last Sabbath. "It was *said* John was not a Catholic, unlike his parents and brothers, and *this* fact had divided them," an assertion for which the *Weekly American* could not find "valid or reasonable evidence." The newspaper thought it more likely he wished to obtain the meager property "by murdering his way to the heirship," although it was unclear what would be left if he had carried out his plan of arson.

A week after Fitzgerald's arrest, the *Auburn Advertiser* believed he seemed "thoroughly convinced of the horrible enormity of the crime of which he is guilty, and the commission of which he freely and fully confesses. He is in a perfect agony of mind, and spends most of his time in the perusal of the Scriptures, and in audible prayer. He weeps very much, groans frequently and loudly, makes self-accusations of his folly and his guilt, and gives every outward manifestation of repentance.—At his own request, Rev. Mr. Ives visited him this morning, and had a protracted interview with him." The substance of this exchange was never revealed, but any remorse or desire for salvation that may have stirred within the prisoner died a quick death or was concealed from view behind a façade of juvenile bravado, as no further mention was made of any such emotional outpourings.

ON SEPTEMBER 16, FITZGERALD'S case came before the grand jury in Auburn, with witnesses from Sterling in attendance. He was indicted for murder in the first degree, and his trial was set to take place before the court of Oyer and Terminer.

On January 1, 1856, Fitzgerald wrote to an acquaintance living in his former neighborhood, "upon whom he thought he had some claim," asking for thirty-five dollars. He wanted it sent to him immediately, to buy some clothes. If anyone thought he was going into court with such a shabby dress, he said, "they were d----y mistaken." Receiving no response, he wrote an even more urgent request on the tenth. He added he wanted to send to Syracuse for a lawyer, as there were none in Auburn fit to manage his case. This letter also went unanswered, but a short time before the trial, Pat sent him seven dollars.

January 30, two days before Fitzgerald was brought into court, Pat, a "legal gentleman" and the person to whom he had written visited him in his cell to transact some business with him. They found the prisoner "in a surly mood, walking the platform on the second tier of cells, with boots blacked and hair oiled, so that both shone with unusual lustre." The lawyer called him by name and asked him to come down. Fitzgerald complied and entered a discussion about the approaching trial. He said he was tired of "staying in that place," wanted to have the matter ended at once and the quicker he was hanged, the better. At this, Pat, whom Fitzgerald had not acknowledged, burst into tears. Fixing his "fiendish eyes" on his sibling, Fitzgerald exclaimed, "Pat, why in hell do you want to make such a fool of yourself!" He then asked the lawyer to accompany him to a part of the jail where he would be out of his brother's sight. The lawyer admitted that he was reluctant at first to be alone with the murderer but followed him:

> *When thus alone, his eye met the cold gaze of* Fitzgerald, *and it struck him as good opportunity to make an impression. He softened his eye—gave him an affecting look, and spoke to him in a tremulous voice.—The hardened boy repeated the remark about his brother, adding that he made a great fool of himself whenever he came to the jail. The gentleman replied, tenderly, "You must make some allowance for Pat. He has no father, no mother, and no brother, save yourself, and he cannot long expect to have you. He is left alone in the world. You must think of these things in regard to Pat."*
>
> *At this the murderer seemed to quail.—The thoughts suggested touched a chord in his heart, which had so long appeared to be crusted over, and beyond reach. But, discovering that an advantage had been gained over him, his visage instantly resumed its cold and hardened expression, and he with emphasis responded—*"Does he think he's agoing to make it any better?" *Our friend replied that he supposed not—that it couldn't be made better. The deed had been consummated, and there was now no help for it.*

In the lawyer's opinion, Fitzgerald, having been disappointed with regard to the money and so on, "would have put his brother out the way in a moment" if given the opportunity. "His desperation seemed to be unbounded, and his determination reckless."[23]

FITZGERALD WAS ARRAIGNED BEFORE Justice Wells on Friday, February 1, represented by Christopher Morgan (William Seward's former law partner), W. Allen of Auburn and Joshua Spencer of Utica. District Attorney Pomeroy, aided by George Rathbun, would conduct the case for the people. The *Auburn Daily American* tersely characterized Fitzgerald's counsel as "able" and did not guess the nature of the plea they would set forth. "The prisoner is an enigma to all."[24]

The murderer "displayed a most astonishing indifference with regard to his crime, its consequence, and his own awful situation.—During the investigation before the Coroner, we remember that he sat in the same room in which three ghastly corpses lay—all side by side, in a bed, with a sheet thrown over them—and manifested there a dogged indifference that was truly marvelous. He exhibited less excitement, less interest, less horror, than any of those present, who gazed upon the terrible spectacle."[25]

Pat Fitzgerald described the layout of the house and his dash through the neighborhood that August night. He claimed John told him the "negroes" had run down the road, contradicting the testimony of other witnesses. Pat had not seen anyone on the road or about the premises; in fact, he had not seen anyone outside the family after he went to bed until O'Neil came. He affirmed that John had sworn more than once that he would kill their father.

O'Neil, Glenn and O'Keefe recalled the tableau of the murder. O'Keefe included the exchange at McEackron's in which Fitzgerald threatened to kill

Former congressman and secretary of state of New York Christopher Morgan (1808–1877), one of three attorneys on the Fitzgerald defense team. *From* Historical Records of a Hundred and Twenty Years, Auburn, N.Y. *(1913).*

his father. "His manner was harsh. I gave him advice; he didn't listen to it very well." William McFarland Jr. recounted Fitzgerald's queries about strychnine, which was also the subject of a conversation they'd had on August 31 at Constable Irwin's house. "He requested me to go into a pantry with him; I went in with him; the door was closed; there was something about the murder, and he requested me to get him some strychnine; he said he wished he had some. I told him I couldn't get it for him conscientiously." (No doubt Fitzgerald had a plan that would spare the county the expense of a trial.) While Fitzgerald was working at his house, he had said more than once "he would be the means" of his father, and any mention of him aroused his anger. Other witnesses testified that Fitzgerald vowed to be the death of his father if he took his wages—or, as Albert Ostrander told it, "damn him if he takes any wages I will take his life." Ostrander repeated a conversation in which Fitzgerald promised to "murder the whole damned kit of Catholics over there" if his father got in his path. He told Fitzgerald if he didn't like the Catholics he ought not to have any personal antipathy against his parents—"he made me an answer that he knew that."

No witnesses were called for the defense, and not one of the attorneys representing the defendant presented an argument. That the jury would decide the prosecution did not prove guilt beyond a reasonable doubt was the best they could hope for. It was left to the court to point out the circumstantial nature of the case:

> *It is one of the most revolting cases that ever came under my observation; in fact gentlemen it is the most horrible case that the annals of jurisprudence give any sketch of. A most heart rending and appalling tragedy, yea.....No one saw it done. Patrick Fitzgerald was called as a witness, and here gentlemen I admit that his evidence is clear, that he was there, no one can doubt....*
>
> *I shall not go over the sickening scene....The point is, gentlemen, who done this bloody deed; one witness tells you of the prisoner's speaking of the n----rs, and seeking to evade the bloody scene, and suspicion of those that were there, the blood on his clothes, his previous threats are all legitimate facts from which you are to draw your conclusion, for if you convict the prisoner, you must do it upon circumstantial evidence. This is as well sometimes, as the facts themselves...in addition to aid these facts, the proof of a very strong hostile feeling on the part of the prisoner at the Bar towards his father previous to this horrible murder, is evidence for you to look upon with a jealous eye. Now gentlemen does your minds rest upon any one else who could have committed this bloody deed besides the prisoner at the Bar; are there any facts connected with evidence in this case that would implicate any one else.*
>
> *It is hardly credible that any human being could have been so lost to natural ties and affections as to commit this triple murder....Are you satisfied by your own convictions which have been inside upon your minds by listening to these appalling facts from the witnesses, that the prisoner at the Bar is the guilty one?...As to the sympathies that are due the prisoner you have nothing to do with at all; you are but the instruments of the law, to do justice, but still we would be glad if some unmistakable evidence could be produced to relieve us of that uncertainty which hangs around circumstantial evidence which sometimes go to a jury.*

Twenty minutes after the jury retired to deliberate, it returned to court. The foreman announced that they had found the prisoner guilty. Fitzgerald was remanded to jail to await his sentence.

"During the whole trial the Prisoner was not moved in the least," observed the *Auburn Daily American*. "Neither did the verdict of the jury start him in his chair, he left the Court room in a swaggering manner, bidding defiance, in his countenance, to the whole Bar of Justice."[26]

Fitzgerald was brought into the crowded, breathlessly silent courtroom on February 8 and seated within the bar, a few feet from the bench. The district attorney moved that sentence be pronounced, and the judge told Fitzgerald to stand up. He did so, with all eyes on him:

> *He met the gaze of all, unmoved and unabashed. Awful as was the situation he occupied, yet he seemed to be the most unconcerned of all those present. He was dressed with scrupulous neatness. It was evident that he had bestowed minute attention to his costume. His dark hair, which he wears in profusion, was combed and curled with great care. His neck was enveloped in a silk check scarf, the ends of which fell so low as almost to conceal his shirt-bosom.—His frock coat was spotless, buttoned in front, and a white handkerchief was visible in the side-pocket. A pair of dark pants and well polished boots completed his "outer man."*[27]

When asked if he had anything to say, Fitzgerald, his eyes fixed on the judge, replied, "Not anything at all, sir." The judge continued:

> *The circumstances of your offence are unparalleled in atrocity in the annals of crime. They evince a degree of depravity and hardihood so revolting, that the mind instinctively revolts from their contemplation. That a man of your age, situated as you were, could coolly and deliberately, in the still hour of the night, with the deadly axe in your hands, steal upon your sleeping victims, and enter upon and complete this horrid work of butchery, without a show of excuse or palliation, and those victims your nearest kindred, your own flesh and blood, would be too much to believe, were it not for the clear and irrefragable evidence, which leaves no doubt of your guilt.*
>
> *You are doubtless aware of the awful doom which now awaits you. In a few moments the judgment of this Court will have been finally passed upon you, and its duty discharged. Before that is done, we would, if it would be possible, awaken you from that insensibility of feeling, in which you seem to have been sunken, from the time you first meditated these foul and unnatural murders, until you were remanded to prison after the jury had pronounced you guilty, to some just and proper sense of your condition, and induce you at once to set about the work of preparation, as far as may be, to stand at that great and solemn tribunal, before which you are now so soon to appear.*

Great and aggravated as is your crime, God's mercy is still greater, and may be obtained, even by you, if sincerely and earnestly sought for with deep penitence and humble reliance upon the atoning blood of the Redeemer.

Think, then, of what you have done. Bring back before your mind your aged parents, as they lay there sleeping, while you, who were indebted to them for your existence, whom they nurtured, protected and cared for from your helpless infancy, stood before them with the deadly weapon and more deadly purpose! Did you not hesitate? Did you not tremble? And when the parricidal blow had fallen upon your poor old father, and your mother aroused from her slumber, and you looked upon her as she raised herself in bed, did not your heart relent? Was there not, at that awful moment, some faltering on your part? What demon then unnerved your arm? Oh think of it! Think of that mother who bore you, who nursed and cradled you in infancy, and had bestowed upon you a mother's love during all your life—what foul fiend could have possessed, and impelled you on, to stain your soul with her life-blood?

And when you turned away from the heart rending spectacle of the lifeless bodies of both your parents, murdered in cold blood by you, was you afraid that your innocent young brother, who still lay sleeping upon the lounge in the same room might, if suffered to live, become a swift witness against you? Had you never entertained affection for James? Had your heart never been warmed towards him with a brother's love? When, from time to time, as you have returned home to the paternal roof, has he not manifested joy at seeing you, and joined with the rest of the domestic circle in your cordial welcome? It is impossible to believe that there has been occasions like these when you must have experienced the sympathies of our common nature. Think then, how, in one fearful and desperate moment, with your hands still reeking in the blood of your murdered parents, with ruthless violence you struck him down, and quenched forever his young life. And remember your only surviving brother who will soon be left alone to mourn, in desolation of heart, the sad havoc you have made. Think how his life must be embittered by the recollection of a father and mother and brother murdered, and you executed upon the gallows, a victim to the violated majesty of the law. . . .

Do not, I beseech you, deceive yourself for one moment with the hope of pardon here, or a commutation of the death penalty. There is not the slightest ground for such a hope. The law which you have violated, is inexorable in its demand. Nothing can expiate your unparalleled guilt but your own violent and ignominious death. The veil of eternity is soon to be drawn aside for you, when you will pass away from this world, and appear, with an assembled universe at the great and final judgment. Think you that you can there meet your parents and brother with composure, without a friend to shelter you from their accusing gaze.

We would not, if we could, unnecessarily harrow your feelings. We desire only to make you sensible of your condition, and would rejoice to see you humble and penitent, before our last sad duty is discharged. Take these parting words in kindness. They are said to you in kindness and in the hope that when you are taken back to prison you will ponder them earnestly.

It only remains for the Court to pronounce upon you the judgment of the law, which is; That you be taken to the prison from whence you last came, and that on Friday [sic] *the 28th of March next you be taken to the place of execution and on that day between the hours of ten o'clock in the forenoon and four o'clock in the afternoon, that you be hung by the neck until you shall be dead; and may the lord have mercy on your soul.*

And now farewell! until you and the Court and this assembled audience shall meet at the resurrection.

"I am much obliged to you sir!" Fitzgerald shot back, casually taking his seat. The *Weekly American* observed that the judge had

exhausted language and ingenuity in an attempt to arouse [Fitzgerald] *to a realizing sense of the enormity of his monstrous crime and its awful consequences; but his efforts utterly failed. While all in the court-room were powerfully moved—not a few even to tears—yet* Fitzgerald *stood unmoved throughout the trying scene. Not a muscle moved. His countenance was bold, hardened in every feature, and his eye was cold as marble....*

We have seen men executed; we have seen them ascend the scaffold with trembling knees, blanched cheeks, streaming eyes, and with prayers trembling upon their white lips; and we have seen them hung by their necks until they were dead. These spectacles were awful, but not to be compared with the scene in the court-room this morning. A mere boy, standing up and receiving sentence of death for the murder of his aged parents and young brother, and yet passing through the awful ordeal as unconcerned as a brute, was to us a sight more horrible than any execution it has ever been our lot to witness.

The *Auburn Daily Advertiser*, also pierced by the words that had could not have affected the defendant any less if they had been spoken in Sanskrit, provided a finishing stroke that surely would have shattered the *American's* consternation threshold: "Fitzgerald left the Court room breathing the most horrid imprecations upon the Judge, District Attorney, Jurors and witnesses, and especially against his only surviving brother who appeared as a witness on the part of the People."[28]

TIME DID NOTHING TO mitigate the vengefulness that consumed Fitzgerald after his sentence: "He often stated that if he could only manage to kill his brother Patrick, he should be perfectly satisfied to die the next hour."[29]

Fitzgerald received regular visits from Reverend B.I. Ives of the Methodist Episcopal Church, occasional ones from Reverend Dr. Cressy of the Episcopal Church and at least one from Reverend Cavanaugh of the Catholic Church. None of the clergyman made the slightest impression on him. "On the contrary, he usually treated their admonitions with levity, and…often made sport of them after their visits."[30]

With his execution a week away, Fitzgerald had yet to betray any sign of remorse or concern over his approaching fate, of which he spoke with equal flippancy. Whether he thought it was deserved may be an equivocal matter. He had remarked to the *Weekly American's* lawyer friend that the men who pronounced him guilty were "the d---dest jury he ever saw" and "they wasn't fit to set on the case of a dog!" He added emphatically, "They wasn't out more'n five minutes—not long enough to know whether they agreed upon a verdict or not!"

When his remaining hours on earth had reached the double digits, Fitzgerald asked for a can of oysters, remarking that "he was determined to live well until his time was up. He also begged for a pack of cards. Of course he did not get them."[31]

Even if this display of perfect insouciance were an act, it left the *Daily American* stunned to the core. "How is it possible for a human being, under the circumstances in which Fitzgerald is placed, to affect or really to care so little about his fate, we are unable to conceive," the publication editorialized on March 21. "This feeling of indifference cannot be human, but rather, on the contrary, fiendish and brutal. Whether Fitzgerald will keep up this spirit of indifference to the last is a question.—That event will settle it. His crime is certainly one of the most unparalleled on record, and his course since has been equally so."

ON MARCH 27, A "large number" of citizens crowded into the hall to see Fitzgerald. Of some of them he demanded twenty-five cents for the privilege, and on one occasion, he said that in order to dispatch business more quickly, and as he had but a short time to stay, he would "show himself to the crowd for one dollar." Most of the money thus collected was distributed among the other prisoners.[32]

In conversation with one of his visitors, "Fitzgerald coolly remarked that there was a prospect of a thaw, and added that he was sorry for it, as he had hoped to take a sleigh-ride to-morrow (to-day) dead or alive. He said that perhaps he should ride down to the State Prison. This showed that his mind was upon a commutation which he had always said he hoped would not be granted."[33]

Before sitting for his daguerreotype, Fitzgerald tended to his toilette assiduously. "His hair was curled with the greatest precision, and his Byron collar carefully adjusted." On his way to the room, he unavoidably passed the gallows erected for his execution. "The ropes and pullies [sic] were all in their proper order, and as his eye fell upon them, a slight change in his countenance was observed." After taking his seat, Fitzgerald struggled for several moments to control his mirth. "Two or three times he burst into immoderate fits of laughter, and finally told the company that unless they all got out of his sight he would not be able to keep a straight face."[34]

Charles Morris of Penn Yan took several images of the condemned youth, one or two of which he kept. The *Penn Yan Democrat* found the subject "a remarkably good looking fellow; the countenance, as seen in the picture, evince no sign of the murderous and reckless disposition that his deed and actions showed him possessed of."[35]

A messenger arrived that evening to convey Fitzgerald's body to his former home for burial, by the side of his murdered parents and brother. He conversed with the prisoner, who asked him why Patrick did not come for him. Patrick was ill and not able to ride so far, he was told. Fitzgerald remarked his brother ought to drown himself in the lake for appearing as a witness against him. He requested a decent burial and said that he "did not want the damn doctors to steal his body."

Sheriff Knapp, in order to conduct a thorough search for weapons or poison, removed Fitzgerald to another cell. The prisoner had often threatened suicide, saying the sheriff "would never have the pleasure of twitching him up."[36] Fitzgerald, enraged by the relocation, "gave vent to his passions in the most horrid oaths, and when remonstrated with by the clergyman who was present, he exclaimed, 'God damn it, it's enough to make any man swear.'"

A search of his cell resulted in the discovery of a case-knife, "well sharpened and made on the edge into a fine saw."[37] Fitzgerald was closely guarded that night, and it was reported that he slept soundly. Upon going to bed, he told his keepers he would be damned if he was going to sit up to keep them company.

According to the *Auburn Weekly American*, "the heartless recklessness of the prisoner was preserved almost until the very last moment, and his firmness never deserted him." The morning of March 28, he danced and sang in his cell, "and no one would have dreamed that he knew he was within a few hours of Eternity." When one of the attendants entered his cell soon after he had bathed, dressed himself and eaten breakfast, "he made no allusion whatever to the dreadful trial that was so near at hand, but playfully offered to wrestle with him!"[38]

To the *Daily Advertiser*, "this hardened wretch appeared more desperate than ever. His language was of the most obscene and blasphemous character. He repeatedly called to the other prisoners, telling them that he was ready, winding up with the exclamation, '*Hangman, drive on your cart!*'" He was asked to prepare to receive two clergymen that morning, who would remain with him until his execution. He replied that no damn clergyman would be admitted to his cell that day.

That morning, the sheriff tested the strength of the gallows by attaching a weight of 180 pounds to the drop rope and touching the spring, whereupon the weight was jerked from the floor and suspended in the air. "Fitzgerald managed to witness this experiment by looking through the key hole of his cell door. He called loudly to the sheriff, and remarked that 'that was done well—it operates first rate.'"[39]

"We mention these things for the purpose of showing our readers what a hardened and unthoughtful wretch the prisoner proved himself to be," the *Daily Advertiser* clarified. "He was certainly the most desperate culprit we ever saw. We hope for the sake of humanity that there are no more like him. In reading all these details it should be borne in mind that the prisoner was a mere youth—being only 19 years of age."

Soon after one o'clock, the Willard Guards, upon the order of the sheriff, marched to the courthouse and took up their station between that building and the jail. Some 1,500 people congregated around the jail, despite the fast-falling snow and wintry air. The crowd "demonstrated fully the morbid curiosity of the people. They could see nothing, hear nothing, and yet they stood for hours about the jail."[40]

Around 2:00 p.m., the representatives of the *Weekly American*, along with a number of other unidentified people, were admitted into Fitzgerald's cell. When they entered, he was standing on the windowsill, shouting to the crowd outside. He was dressed in gaiter boots, dark pants and shirt, *sans* coat and vest. His hair was combed and "oiled with scrupulous care." He appeared "somewhat nervous, but not much excited." He jumped down from the windowsill, turned "with a gay and reckless air" to his company and entered into conversation with the Honorable Morgan, Dr. Hyde and others present whom he knew. He laughed at the crowd outside, which he could see from his window, "standing and receiving the pitiless peltings of the storm. Who could have thought *he* was the victim for whom the halter and gallows were prepared within a few feet of where he stood, and who was in a few minutes to suffer death?"

The *Weekly American* reporter found the interview "a curious one. There was a young man, in the first blush of manhood, standing upon the very threshold of eternity."

"Did you sleep well last night, John?"

"Yes sir!"

"Do you wish to see or converse with a clergyman?"

"No *sir!* I don't feel well." He pointed to his heart, and the doctor examined him. The pulse was beating rapidly.

In reply to a question, he said he would like to "take a little chloroform, if it would be of any use, but as for bleeding he regarded it as only torture, and if allowed to do so, would not submit to it. He said he wished to submit to no torture *while he lived*."

"John, if the Governor should come now and commute your sentence to imprisonment for life, would you like it?"

"No sir! I would step right out and pull hemp in preference. I had rather be hung than go to prison for life!" Here he added that if the sheriff would fix the springs to the gallows so that he could reach it, he would hang himself. He stated the sheriff and his attendants had treated him kindly, and then, for a few moments, "seemed much disturbed and nervous."

A doctor asked him if he objected to giving up his body for dissection. The *Weekly American* reporter was shocked at this inquiry, but Fitzgerald laughed loudly. "No sir! *You* would look pretty cutting up my body!"

Upon the announcement that a clergyman wished to see him, he said, "If he comes in here he'll get my fist—that's all! What good can he do me *now?* I don't want him."

In response to an "earnest appeal" to forgive his brother, Fitzgerald said he had kind words only for those who had been kind to him since he had been in prison. Apparently, this did not include his brother, whom he refused to forgive. He said perhaps he would after the rope was around his neck, and he stretched up, but not before.

"Go ahead! You can kill me—that's *all* you can do! Can't you arrange the hanging so that I can touch it off myself? I want to die; I'm tired of jail life, any way."

At 2:05 p.m., Reverend Ives, who had been with Fitzgerald in the morning, in company with Dr. Cressy, returned alone and requested to see him. At the time, Fitzgerald was conversing with Morgan, but after "a few moments reflection," he agreed to see the reverend.

All spectators except Morgan left the cell. "We did not after that exchange a word with the prisoner. Happening to see us using a small note book and pencil, he became much incensed, and wished to know whether we were 'taking down' everything he said."

Ives and Morgan conversed with Fitzgerald until 2:35 p.m., when Ives "offered up to the throne of grace a most touching and eloquent prayer," during which the prisoner "manifested some little feeling," even shedding tears, but Ives informed the *Daily Bulletin* that "his spirit was not subdued. He still averred that he would never forgive his brother."

Those whom the sheriff had invited to be present as witnesses and deputies, about forty in all, assembled in the jail corridor. The gallows, arranged so that the noose hung about three feet from the floor, directly at the entrance to the apartment, was examined with "much curiosity."[41]

At 3:00 p.m., the sheriff entered the hall and said that the prisoner requested "that not a word should be uttered after he was brought in, and that the execution should proceed in silence." Two minutes later, Fitzgerald entered the corridor, wearing a floor-length white gown over his pants and boots. His hair was dressed with customary meticulousness. Amid "profound silence," he was placed beneath the noose. "He was apparently cool, firm, and bore himself bravely at that dreadful moment." As the breathless spectators watched, his arms were pinioned and his wrists bound. "He stood firm and unmoved.—He did not quail, even at that awful moment. We noticed that his fingers twitched a little, and that he twirled his thumbs some, but there was no exclamation, no prayer, no sob, no sigh, no repentance. Truly, truly, it was an awful spectacle!"[42]

While a deputy bound his arms, "he took umbrage at something that was done" and exclaimed, "Gentlemen! Don't torture me—hang me, if you want to!" Immediately after he was pinioned, Fitzgerald looked up at the rope suspended above him, shook his head and remarked, "It is pretty hard, boys."

He motioned for Morgan to approach and in a whisper asked if chloroform could be administered to him. "The reply, of course, was in the negative. He never spoke again."[43]

The white cap was drawn over his head and the rope placed around his neck. At 3:06 p.m., the rope was cut, and the drop of a three-hundred-pound weight violently jerked Fitzgerald about three feet from the floor. He barely struggled, and only a "few convulsive movements about the chest" were visible.[44] In less than six minutes, the physicians pronounced him dead. An examination revealed that the neck was dislocated at the first vertebra. After hanging the required time, he was cut down and his body taken to the hall of the courthouse, through which 1,500 to 2,000 people traipsed to view it.

According to the *Oswego Palladium*, Fitzgerald's remains were taken to Sterling for interment; public sentiment refused to permit their burial in a graveyard, and they were deposited in a nearby field. "During the ensuing night the body was 'snatched' and carried off for dissection, no doubt."

The *Weekly American* praised the sheriff for the perfection with which he prepared to discharge "his painful and terrible duty" and the Willard Guards, who kept the slightly noisy crowd under subjection. Plaudits out of the way, the newspaper then offered a requiescat for Fitzgerald that all but spat on his grave:

> *Murder is adjuged* [sic] *to be a capital crime. Hanging the murderer for the commission of the crime of Murder, is a dreadful thing to witness.*
>
> *It was our lot to see* Fitzgerald *hung today. He has passed to his account! The deed is done! May the God who is over us all have mercy upon his soul!*
>
> *Thus has closed a direful tragedy. He shed man's blood, and by man his blood has been shed!*
>
> *Fitzgerald will be remembered through all time to come as the most atrocious murderer whose name stains the annals of crime in our country. At the dead of night, deliberately, and therefore with full knowledge of the monstrous atrocity of the act, he seized an axe and butchered, in cold blood, his* father, *his* mother *and his* brother!—*There is no parallel to this work of heartless, fiendish murder....*
>
> *In relation to the unhappy wretch who has just passed from time to eternity, it is painful to know that to the very last he remained unrepentant and obdurate, and that his conduct throughout his long imprisonment, and especially since his trial and conviction, has been such as to awaken in no*

mind the least emotion or sympathy,—Should we relate what we know of his conduct during the last hours of his guilty life, we should only shock the feelings of our readers. Suffice it to say—he remained callous to the last, and displayed the most amazing evidence of depravity and fiendishness.

As we have said, he has passed to his account! The grave has closed over him!—The earth hides from its surface one of the most apparently heartless creatures that ever bore the human form. Let us forget him.—He has expiated the awful crime in death the most dreadful and ignominious known to the laws of our country. Let the pall of oblivion cover him forever!

Chapter 3

WILLIAM FEE

Galen, Wayne County
1859

Around 5:00 p.m. on Sunday, September 25, 1859, a woman between the ages of twenty-five and thirty-five entered the yard of Mrs. Casey's boardinghouse, about six miles east of the village of Clyde in the town of Galen. Sarah Fuller, a resident of Crusoe Island, was the first to encounter the stranger. She told Fuller she had come from the east, was too tired to travel any farther and asked if she could stay the night. Casey said, "Tell the lady to come in and rest a few minutes."

The woman said she was Irish but did not give her name. Her English was good, "not broguey," in Fuller's words. She had worked for three "Yankee" families and had received only a dollar from them. She claimed she had slept on a pile of boards the night before and had unsuccessfully applied to a Yankee family to keep her overnight. If Casey did not allow her to stay, she would have to spend another night outside. Casey could not accommodate her, as she had male boarders. The woman then asked where she could get work and was told it was not far to Mr. Armitage's, where she would find employment. Despite her fatigue, the woman said she would go to Armitage's; if she couldn't get work there, she inquired, could she come back and stay overnight? Fuller told her she could.

While the stranger passed out of the house into the yard, William Fee of Lock Pit, a twenty-three-year-old Irish-born canal laborer, entered the dwelling and asked Casey for a drink. While she was getting it for him, the woman left the yard. Casey said to Fee, "There goes a woman you can have for company."

"Where?" asked Fee. Casey pointed in the direction the woman had gone.

"Come on," Fee said to his co-worker Thomas Muldoon, starting after the woman. She had gone only a few rods west toward the old canal bridge, half a mile from Casey's house, on which two men, Prosser Jones and Abram Fitch, were shooting at ducks.

Before the woman reached the bridge, Fee took hold of her, and she said, "Let me be." Jones didn't hear Fee's reply. Muldoon said, "Come on good lady, we mind our business and trouble no one."

When they came on the bridge, Muldoon asked the woman what she was looking for. "A boat," she answered. Muldoon said, "Let's go," and the woman proceeded on her way.

Muldoon suggested she might be a virtuous woman. Fee said he had seen many such towpath agents—that she (here Jones's testimony was replaced by asterisks) and that was all he wanted. Fee said, "Let's see which way she goes, but go which way she will, we — — her or she will die." Fee and Muldoon waited until she had crossed the bridge, and then Fee followed her along what Jones called "the lonely road no one travels." The men trailed her closely for a way; then, in the swamp some ninety rods from the bridge, Fee grabbed her from behind and threw her out of Jones's sight. He heard two screams, and after seeing no one for two or three minutes, Jones started toward them.

At that moment, they came into his sight, the woman first. Fee came toward Jones and said, "Fire!"

"What shall I fire at?" asked Jones.

Fee's reply to that escaped Jones's memory, but his next words were, "What did I tell you? Didn't I tell you I'd — — and I have!"

Fee asked Jones to go back with him. Jones refused. Fee backed up slightly and said, "Hurrah." He stayed where he was for a few minutes, went a little farther, sat down, got up and moved on west out of Jones's sight.

During this time, the woman passed around the turn of the road, heading west, with Muldoon following her. Once again they disappeared from Jones's sight, and he saw no more of them. He returned to the bridge, where he and Fitch waited for about twenty minutes for ducks to appear before heading home.

ON THE WARM, BRIGHT Monday morning of September 26, Bradley Thompson, the contractor on a section of the canal, was on his way to

Crusoe Island when he found the woman's lifeless body by the roadside on the turnpike, some eighty rods from the bridge. She lay on her right side, her head in the hollow of a stump. Her disheveled hair hung over her neck and shoulders and partly obscured her pale face. Her eyes were slightly open and glassy. The purplish-red fabric of her old, soiled calico dress was torn across the front, exposing her breasts. Some pieces of the garment were gone, others shredded, the hooks and eyes torn off and straightened. A carpetbag and large red shawl lay nearby. A pink checked apron covered her knees and portions above and below them. Her feet, placed close together, were bare and caked with dried mud.

Thompson, frightened at the sight, did not venture near the body. He turned to his teenage companion, George West, to discuss whether they should go back or continue on to the island. When Nathan Fitch (father of Abram and father-in-law of Jones) approached in a wagon, they told him there was a corpse in the swamp.

While Thompson and West headed for the island, Fitch thought of turning back but decided to go on. Driving very slowly, he passed the body, taking all the notice he could of it. He did not stop, however, as he had two female passengers and "thought the sight of a dead woman too ridiculous for them." He noticed the victim had a wound, apparently a cut, on her face. He requested a third party to ask Mr. Armitage to send for the coroner.

Summoned by Armitage, Dr. H.D. Whitlock took charge of the body, which he found eight or ten feet from the center of the road. He thought the corpse looked like it had been moved a little. He found a fresh cut over the right eye, about three-fourths of an inch long, parallel to the eyebrow. There was a slight cut over the nose, a bruise on the cheek and a discolored spot as large as a half dollar under the right eye, as might have been caused by a blow from a blunt instrument. Three finger marks encircled the left side of her considerably enlarged neck but did not come near the front of the throat. Her right leg was swollen, bruised and discolored. One knee, a thigh and the underclothes bore traces of blood. When Dr. Darwin Colvin arrived shortly thereafter and helped him move the body, they discovered the feces had been evacuated.

The deceased was placed in a wagon and taken to Clyde. The doctors brought along her satchel, which was found to contain several articles of clothing, a pair of shears and knitting needles. The next day, Drs. Colvin, Neely and Weed were summoned to hold a postmortem examination. Her uterus contained a small amount of blood, apparently menstrual fluid, and her lungs were "heavy and loaded to their fullest extent with blood of a dark color, almost black."[45] The trachea under the finger marks was not injured. The examiners found no evidence of recent "sexual connection"[46] in the vagina or uterus and no seminal fluid in the latter. At the coroner's inquest, the physicians expressed the opinion that strangulation was the cause of death.

Based on the testimony of the two witnesses (who, the *Syracuse Daily Journal* noted, had apparently not gone "to the relief of the woman or paid any further attention to the matter"), the jury returned a verdict that the victim came to her death by violence at the hands of Fee, supposedly with assistance from Muldoon. Neither of these men had appeared for work Monday morning.

QUITE BY ACCIDENT, BRIAN O'Connor, a contractor at Clyde, came across Fee in New York City on October 15. The men fell into conversation, and under the pretense of finding a drinking place, O'Connor led Fee into several stores and shops until he found a policeman, whom he directed at once to arrest Fee. A telegraph to Sheriff Adrastus Snedaker of Wayne County announced Fee's apprehension, and a deputy sheriff was sent for him. The citizens of Clyde, according to the *Syracuse Central City Courier*, were with difficulty "restrained from lynching Fee, so indignant were they at the outrage perpetrated by this scoundrel." Muldoon was arrested in Scranton, Pennsylvania, and brought to jail Saturday evening. "These worthies will probably pay the penalty of their crimes upon the gallows," the *Courier* predicted.

Residents of the vicinity readily accepted that Fee and Muldoon were the perpetrators. Their bad reputations, coupled with their disappearance from the area, did nothing to underscore the presumption of innocence. Fee seemed an especially likely culprit; according to the *Rochester Union*, "his conduct was bad, and he was for three or four years, or since the family have resided there, the terror of all who knew him, and his relatives do not bear a favorable character."

The grand jury preferred indictments against Fee and Muldoon for murder. They were arraigned on October 28 and pleaded not guilty, "whereupon they were taken back to close confinement."[47]

FEE'S TRIAL BEGAN ON Monday, January 30, 1860, with Justice Knox presiding. Attorney General Myers of Albany appeared that evening, and the next morning, he took a seat with the counsel for the people, consisting of Wayne

County district attorney Jacob Decker of Red Creek and J.D. Husbands of Rochester. Stephen Williams of Newark and Colonel J.H. Martindale and L. Farrar, both of Rochester, represented the defendant.

Seats were "at a premium," according to the *Lyons Republican*, and most of the audience retained theirs during the noon recess. Others sold theirs for prices as high as fifty cents. Knox thoughtfully assigned seats behind his desk to reporters.

Husbands, opening the case for the prosecution, spoke for nearly an hour "and was listened to with breathless attention by the audience," noted the *Republican*.

Thompson and Nathan Fitch described the circumstances under which they'd found the dead woman, and Whitlock minutely detailed the condition of her body. Fee's counsel objected when Husbands asked Colvin to state whether in his opinion the deceased came to her death from natural causes. When the court allowed Colvin to speak, the witness replied, "I believe she came to her death by strangulation. By strangulation I mean the shutting off by the use of any agent, of atmospheric air either by hanging, ligature or the application of the hand."

On the third day, Jones and Abram Fitch presented their testimony, whereupon the prosecution rested. Williams opened for the defense, stating that although Fee was poor and humble, perhaps even debased, and "the circumstances appeared appalling against" him, the defense "expected to show that the facts and circumstances were consistent with his innocence." Williams contended there was not sufficient evidence to support the theory that the woman died in defense of her virtue; there was no evidence of rape, attempted rape or assault and battery; and it would be proven that immediately upon leaving Jones in the road, Fee went directly home.

The first witness, Dr. Henry Moore of Rochester, stated the woman might have died of epilepsy, "as the appearance after death by that disease and strangulation, are nearly the same." Dr. Weed testified that, outside of the facts of the case, he "should think death was caused by asphyxia, which might have been produced by a variety of means."

James Fee, father of the prisoner, said that William boarded with him at the house the elder Fee kept for men working on the canal. Even though he couldn't tell when his son had gone to bed Sunday, he claimed he'd slept at the house; he had seen William at supper at about 6:30 p.m. At any rate, he was sure William had been home before dark—he had seen him at intervals all evening. He only went a few rods from the house and sat on a pile of stones. When James first heard of the body being found, between 11:00

a.m. and 12:00 p.m. Monday, William, he said, was at work, braking cars for Conway & Slater. He didn't know when he "quit." William had "staid about the home all day, and left sometime that night"—he couldn't tell when. He had seen him at 7:00 p.m. and gave him money, William's own. He left on foot, taking no baggage that James knew of. He did not see in which direction William headed. The next time he saw his son was at the jail in Lyons.

William's brother George, who lived with their father, was sworn next. He had stayed at his father's the night before the body was found, and William had been in the house when George came home. At that time, "it wasn't quite dark," "dusky a little." Some twenty or thirty minutes later, he sat down to supper by candlelight, without William. He went to bed between 8:00 p.m. and 9:00 p.m. and slept with William, who had turned in before he did. When George got up at 4:00 a.m. or 5:00 a.m., William was still abed. He saw the defendant at work on Monday, after 10:00 a.m., and then again at dinner, around 1:00 p.m. He claimed he had seen William between dinner and 10:00 p.m., about the house and "where the cars come down" but not at work. He didn't see him at supper. After William left Monday night, George saw no more of him.

James Fee's tenant John Egan testified that he had taken supper at Fee's Sunday and thought he saw William at 6:00 p.m. or 7:00 p.m. He didn't know the exact time William had eaten supper, as he did not look at a timepiece. On this note, the defense closed.

On Thursday morning, February 2, Martindale began his summation for the defense. The *Republican* deemed him "a ready and attractive speaker, though we think he might have improved his style by omitting a portion of muscular exercise. His only fault is that he is too theatrical."

Martindale's theory was that the woman was a prostitute and "made no attempt to resist Fee's ravishment; that she thereafter stepped upon the front of her skirt, fell down, and was seized with a fit of epilepsy, during which she clutched her own throat and died, leaving the marks of her fingers upon her neck…that the marks upon her face were occasioned by her falling upon the ground or the roots of trees, or that the wounds had been inflicted by a boatman who had the day before (as Fee stated to his counsel the woman told him) put her off a boat." He argued "none but an abandoned woman…would have been in such a place, at such a time, and under such circumstances. He did not attempt to show that Fee did not accomplish his infamous purpose, but based his argument mainly on the theory that Fee *did not know she was dead*, else, he urged, how could he go home and to bed, that night, and to his work next day, with the horrible secret upon his mind?"

The *Republican* found Martindale's four-hour speech "able and elaborate, but whatever the effect may have been upon the Jury, it apparently failed to convince the audience of Fee's innocence, if we may judge from the countenances."

Myers spoke next, with a command of language the *Republican* believed had rarely been equaled. For the next two and a half hours, "he attacked the theory of the defence, and literally tore it to pieces, scattering the argument of Mr. Martindale to the winds. Once or twice (though it was highly improper at such a time and in such a place) the listeners were unable to restrain an expression of their admiration of his oratory and their sympathy with his plea, and greeted the Honorable gentleman with hearty rounds of applause."

The *Republican* noted that the only person seemingly watching the proceedings with indifference was William Fee himself. "We have been unable to detect in his countenance the slightest emotion, and he has appeared more like a stolid looker-on than the person whose life or death depended upon the result of the trial."

Judge Knox charged the jury to rely entirely on legal evidence for a conviction, not Fee's aspect while on trial. They were not to say that God has written murder on his face—that is not so. "He has written no such crime upon any human face, &c." It was said the evidence showed the woman to be a prostitute, but a prostitute as well as a virtuous woman may be raped. Regarding the conversation on the bridge, counsel did not differ as to the meaning of Fee's unprintable words; it was an exaggerated remark, a "slang" phrase, but was "strong evidence that he intended to have sexual intercourse with this woman, that is the most it proves." Did the marks found on her person implicate Fee and Muldoon, or were they the result of natural causes? If they found from the evidence that Fee and Muldoon "were acting in concert to accomplish their object, though but one may have done the deed, both are equally guilty."

The jury withdrew to deliberate. A hat was set on a table into which each man was to place a strip of paper printed with his verdict. The *Republican* gave an account of the proceedings:

No discussion was had, not a word was spoken. Strong men paced the floor in tears earnestly, striving to find one ray of hope for the unfortunate being whom they had in charge,—one shred of evidence or law, by which they might avoid the terrible duty of conviction,—but all in vain. A death-like stillness pervaded the room, nothing being heard but their muffled tramp, and occasionally a deep sigh. It was a trying moment. Now one has deposited his ballot, and retired to a distant corner of the room, conscious of having discharged his duty, gives vent to his feelings in deep drawn sighs, perhaps in tears. After a few moments, another, feeling that he cannot do otherwise deposits his fatal ballot; and so on, until eleven ballots have been cast. The twelfth man could not summon courage sufficient to enable him to write his convictions. An hour and a half was occupied in this balloting. And upon opening the ballots, all of the eleven were found to contain the fatal word GUILTY. The twelfth man concurred with the eleven, and their duty was discharged.

After slightly more than three hours, the jury returned with their verdict. The prisoner "maintained the same stolidity which has characterized his behavior since the commencement of the trial," noted the *Republican*. "He remarked to an officer, with an oath, that it was 'tough,' but he 'wasn't going to lie awake thinking about it.' Does such a creature deserve sympathy?"

Williams moved the suspension of sentence, for the purpose of pursuing a writ error. Court was adjourned to Friday.

The *Republican* found it "proper to remark" that Fee had been "ably and manfully defended. We do not think he could have selected a counsel who would have conducted the defense more carefully, more energetically, or with greater credit to themselves...in fine, nothing that *could* have been done for the poor wretch whose doom is sealed, has been neglected by his counsel."

On Friday afternoon, Judge Knox addressed the prisoner. "William Fee, have you anything to say why the sentence of death should not be passed upon you?"

"Yes sir," said Fee. "I am as innocent of the charge as any man in this house."

Knox proceeded:

I am about to discharge a most melancholy duty, which I pray God I may never again have occasion to perform. The sentence which I am about to pass upon you will for a brief time deprive you of your liberty, and will then consign you to an infamous death, purchased by your crime. You have been indicted for the crime of murder and convicted by a Jury fairly selected and impartial in every respect. They were selected by yourself. Your counsel did not exhaust their peremptory challenges because they were satisfied that it was impartial. The Court, in laying down the law, if they have made any mistake, have made it on your side, and not on that of the People....And the Court would have been glad if you could have given some fact showing a reasonable doubt for your guilt. We have gone to the utmost degree of law in your favor. I leaned toward you in my charge, and gave you the benefit of suggestions not made by your own counsel.—Yet the Jury have found you guilty, and in justice to the Jury and all concerned, we must say that our consciences and our hearts approve of their verdict. We think the evidence of your guilt warranted it.

On Sunday night, time suggestive of very different employments than those in which you were engaged—you seized this lonely destitute woman, exercising your superior force upon her—defenseless and weakened by want of food.

The offence of murder you have aggravated by adding to it the crime of rape—an offence which is thought by some, to be yet more heinous. Most men would prefer to have a wife or daughter taken from them by sudden death, rather than they should fall victims to this revolting outrage. There seems to be no excuse for you. Her very weakness should have been her defense. Your companion, Muldoon, had some sparks of humanity—for he said to you dissuasively, "she may be a virtuous woman." With a declaration unfit to be repeated, except when indispensible in way of evidence, you declared you would have your will of her, or she should lose her life. You did have your will—she lost her life—and you will lose your life.

Now you will go from this place to jail, and from thence to execution. This court cannot pardon you, nor has it any desire to do so, neither can it recommend you to pardon.—The Governor will not pardon you. No power on earth can extricate you from the toils you have wove about you....

You go from this fallible tribune to one which is unerring. There you will meet this victim of your unrestrained passions, and must answer for her blood....

My hope is that, though your sins are red as blood, by proper repentance, you may receive that mercy which God alone, and not this Court, is authorized to extend to you. It but remains for me to pronounce upon you the sentence of the law, which is, that you be taken to the jail from whence you came, and from that place, on Friday, the 23rd day of March next, you be taken to the place of execution, and there hung by the neck until you be dead, and may God Almighty have mercy upon your soul.

The large audience was "almost breathless with attention" during the judge's address, "and we saw tears stealing down many cheeks," noted the *Republican*. "The prisoner struggled for a while to restrain his feelings, but as the Judge pronounced the closing words of the sentence, he burst into an agony of tears, and his sobs were audible throughout the court-room as he was being removed to the jail."

THE *WAYNE DEMOCRAT PRESS* reviewed the evidence against Fee to ascertain whether there was room for doubt as to his guilt. After the first assault, Fee and the woman emerged from a thicket, Fee heading east toward the witnesses and the woman going west, accompanied by Muldoon. The latter were "traveling at a good pace" and passed out of sight around a bend in the road ten minutes before Fee reached that point; the body was found 16 rods (264 feet) west of the bend. "The woman was traveling fast, under the escort of Muldoon, who she evidently looked upon as her protector, for the purpose of getting out of the swamp before Fee should overtake her, yet with strong desire to get out of the way, and the rapid pace at which she was going when last seen, ten minutes time was consumed in getting sixteen rods!" When the woman passed out of sight, she was likely traveling at a rate of three miles per hour. Thus she would have been half a mile west of the bend, and 144 rods west of where her body was found, at the moment Fee reached the bend in the road:

Yet the ten minutes elapsed, and according to the verdict of the jury, Fee overtook the woman and murdered her, within sixteen rods of the spot he passed ten minutes behind her! Now we would like to know how the ten minutes of time were spent by Muldoon and the woman. Certainly it was not consumed in traveling, if it had been they would have been out of harm's way and Fee saved the ignominious death that awaits him.

Had the counsel for the prisoner, instead of assuming ground which evinced his own convictions and shocked and disgusted his hearers, called the attention of the jury to the facts we have narrated (and certainly, he ought not to have overlooked them), could not honest and conscientious men have entertained even more than a doubt of Fee's guilt?

We do not wish to prejudice the public mind against Muldoon. However satisfactorily he may account for the detention of the woman after they got out of sight, he has enough to answer for.

Fee's counsel prepared a "Bill of Exceptions," which was argued before Judge Knox on Saturday, February 25, with the object of allowing the case to be taken to the General Term of the Supreme Court, on an application for a new trial. The *Wayne Democratic Press* stated that the contrition Fee exhibited immediately after his sentence passed as soon as he learned of his counsel's efforts in this matter, "and he relapsed into his habitual profane and vulgar habits."

That week, the final answer was given that deprived Fee of any hope for a reprieve, "if indeed he was ever fully bereft of it," said the *Rochester Union*. "He has never manifested any degree of penitence, while he has not been very obdurate."

The *Lyons Republican*, on the contrary, believed that Fee had been buoyed with hopes of a stay in the proceedings until that time, "but was at last broken down in spirit, and appeared deeply sorrowful and penitent. His appearance was truly affecting."

The gallows were erected and tested at the courthouse on March 20; they were to be moved inside the jail, where, on Friday, March 23, Fee, the "unhappy wretch," would "pay the penalty of his last crime," the *Wayne Democrat Press* reported on March 21. The implication was that Fee could be labeled a career criminal, in accordance with the blackguard status of his relatives; indeed, one of his brothers was then under indictment for assault and battery.

Until the last day or two, Fee "appeared to be destitute of religious feeling," said the *Union*, "and even then he was not softened at heart sufficiently to warrant a hope that he was in a condition to die." Fee's mother was a Catholic, a faith his father vehemently opposed, and the Fee siblings apparently had grown up without any religious education. William had declared himself a Protestant until March 21, and despite Protestant clergymen's frequent visits to the jail to prepare him for death, they left no satisfactory impression on him. His mother, to whom he was deeply attached, conquered the opposition of her husband and then her son, who had repeatedly "disclaimed" her faith to the clergymen during his incarceration. The day before his death, after a meeting with his mother, William made open profession of Catholicism and consented to receive ministrations from Father Constant of Clyde and Father Casey of Palmyra. Representatives of the *Rochester Democrat* who visited the jail at 10:00 p.m. on Thursday found half a dozen Irish girls gathered around the door of Fee's cell, reading to him from the Catholic Prayer Book. A sympathetic visitor, John Cole, found the prisoner "engaged with the Catholic domine" that morning and wrote in his diary, "There has been no such stormy day this winter as today. Snowing, blowing, terrible blowing. A sad day as the last one which Fee will see on earth."[48]

The *Union* claimed that Fee appeared cheerful that day and treated his approaching execution with levity, telling stories to lighten the passing hours. The sheriff asked him to try on a coat he was to wear the next day, and Fee asked, "Am I going to be hung in a new suit of clothes?" When told he would be, Fee replied, "I shall be dressed up and ready to travel, and will go down town about half past four tomorrow." He remarked that he would like to live long enough to see how the great prizefight in England resulted. Two or three days earlier, he told the sheriff, "You'll have a nice time tossing this old body about" and had asked a young man if he was "coming to see him hang, on Friday." His father, mother and brothers took leave of him Thursday, and "the parting was an affecting one, as between the mother and her son." He did not retire to his cell to sleep until nearly midnight.

Questioned by *Democrat* reporters in his cell that same evening, Muldoon had no comment on the subject of the upcoming execution. "If Bill cares to tell anything before he dies, he may—I shan't ask him to; but if he tells the truth and the whole of it I'm not afraid." He said he was "well used" at the jail, with "plenty to eat and drink, and the Sheriff's a real gentleman—but I wish that I was out of this." He said he had known Fee and worked with him for several years, but they had never been intimate; it was only by chance they were together the day the murder was committed. When asked to tell what he knew of Fee's previous history, he shook his head and replied, "No, I'll say nothing of the boy that's going to die."

THE GALLOWS HAD BEEN erected in one of the jail's small halls, to which a maximum of fifty or sixty people could be admitted. The spectators who did not have to join the crowd outside the jail received tickets reading, "Admit the bearer to the execution of William Fee at the Wayne County Jail on March 23, 1860."

Mrs. Fee desired to see her son on Friday morning, but Fee would not consent, saying she could do him no good, and "he feared that he would be broken down in courage to go through the terrible ordeal now approaching so fast."

Correspondents of the *Rochester Democrat* visited the jail at 9:00 a.m. and found the prisoner in conversation with the two priests. Shortly after their arrival, "he partook of the Holy Sacrament." The observers found his appearance "calm and composed," as he had slept soundly the night before,

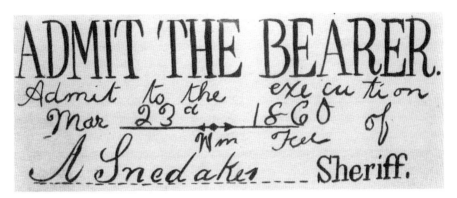

Facsimile of a ticket to William Fee's execution. *Author's collection.*

"and expressed himself willing to die." At Fee's request, they entered the cell and from one of the priests took a statement the prisoner wished to have published after his death:

> *"I die innocent of the murder of the woman. I am not aware that I caused her death. I accept the death to which I am condemned as the atonement for the sins of my life."*
>
> *He wished us to say that he bore no malice to any person living—that he had no wish to live—that he would not accept a pardon, if it were possible to grant one—that he died repentant of his sins, and hoped to meet his friends in another and a better world.*
>
> *He appeared more subdued and broken spirited than we had expected to find him. He expressed much sympathy for Muldoon, and spoke to his attendants respecting his case, saying he hoped Muldoon would be able to prove his innocence and would be acquitted. Fee's face was pale and haggard, and his movements quick and nervous—the shadow of death was upon him, and in the hollow cheeks, the restless motion of the eyes, the thin, transparent pallor of the skin, were but partly revealed the fierce struggle of fear, dread, and, perhaps, remorse, then racking his mind.*

At 1:30 p.m., the sheriff led the procession into the hall. He was followed by Undersheriff Nottingham and then Fathers Casey and Constant, with the prisoner, supported by two officers, bringing up the rear. Fee was dressed in a dark coat, vest and pants along with a turban-like white cap, constructed so that it could be pulled down under his chin, "hiding his features from view at the fatal moment."[49] He walked slowly but appeared composed.

Nottingham read the death warrant while the prisoner stood erect under the noose, swaying back and forth, "as if undergoing great mental agitation,"[50] clutching a white handkerchief in his right hand, his attention focused on the crucifix in his left. The *Lyons Republican* noted that he "preserved a quiet demeanor and listened attentively."

Fee then seated himself in the chair assigned him. The priests knelt before him, and Father Constance read a prayer, which Fee repeated by sentences, "in an audible tone, and with much promptness. All this time a swaying motion backwards and forwards was noticed."[51]

Nottingham said it was his duty to execute the sentence of the law. "William Fee, the time has arrived to put this sentence into execution. Have you anything to say? If so, you have now an opportunity to say what you wish."

"Yes sir, I have," Fee replied. Nottingham told him to say it now. In a firm voice, Fee continued:

> *For the murder of this woman that I shall have to die, I die innocent of murder; and I give my best respects to Mr. Snedaker and Mrs. Snedaker, for they have used me well as long as I have been here. He is a perfect gentleman, and she a perfect lady. Mr. Clark Potts* [the turnkey] *is a perfect gentleman—he has used me well since I have been here. As for my enemies in this world, I pardon them with the greatest of pleasure, and hope God will pardon me.*

The sheriff proceeded to pinion Fee's arms at the elbow with a strap. Fee remarked, as if in some question regarding it, "I don't know how far down it is." He then glanced up at the rope and halter. He asked leave to say one more word. Permission was granted, and he said, "I hope my friends will not throw any reflection upon my partner, Tom Muldoon, when I am no more. There will be no reflection thrown on him—that my folks will throw no reflection on him."

District Attorney Decker asked Fee to repeat what he said about Muldoon—did he mean to say Muldoon was innocent? "Yes, they must not blame him for me being in his company," Fee answered. "God bless the whole of yees boys. That is all I have to say!"

The cap was then drawn over his face. While the halter was adjusted to his neck, Fee said, "Put it on right now—soon be done by and by."

At twelve minutes before two o'clock, the sheriff waved his hand, and a deputy pulled the string that was attached to the foot of another deputy who stood over the gallows. "The latter let the axe fall, and Fee was in an instant jerked from his feet and dangling in the air. The slack of the rope was sufficient to draw him up about three feet, and he settled back about one foot. He struggled somewhat for a few seconds, and muscular motion was quite apparent for several minutes. The halter drew up the knot to the back of the neck, but did not break it." His pulse at the wrist ceased to beat after eight minutes; after twenty minutes, his heart was still. "He died of strangulation, and died easily no doubt."[52]

After the body had been suspended for half an hour, it was taken down, laid out and placed in a coffin. "The appearance of the corpse was in no way repulsive, the countenance having a rather pleasant look," commented the *Rochester Union*.

Besides the officers, about one hundred people witnessed the execution. None of Fee's relatives was present. Snedaker had detailed the Lyons Light Guard the night before, patrolling the grounds on horseback to preserve order. According to the *Lyons Republican*, "Scores of over-curious persons collected outside, anxious to hear and see all that was possible, with a thick stone wall between them and the scene within. Many of these would-be sight-seers took their places as early as nine o'clock, and maintained it until the execution was over." When Fee's death was announced to the restless crowd, the news received "thunderous applause and the hearty laughter of farmers on a holiday."[53]

The coffin was removed from the gallows room to an adjoining office and set on some chairs, ready to be delivered to the friends who had been waiting in one of the upstairs rooms at the jail. Before the coffin was closed, Fee's parents and two brothers came to look at the corpse. "The mother and one brother gave vent to their emotions by the most agonizing screams, while the father and other brother exhibited more composure. The scene was an affecting one to the few spectators who witnessed it."[54]

At 3:30 p.m., a sleigh transported the coffin to Lock Pit Cemetery for burial. Fee had expressed the desire to be buried on the bank of the river but deferred to his mother's wishes. Watches were set to prevent the removal of the body, which Fee's friends had been led to believe would be attempted. "Doubtless there is no foundation for fear on that score," the *Union* deadpanned.

Rarely did newspapers object to the imposition of death sentences or examine the circumstances leading to murder convictions, and the cocksure *Union* was no exception. "Of his guilt there was no doubt, and of the justice of his sentence there can be no diversity of opinion." Even if Fee were innocent of murder, he "ravished this woman, and for that crime deserved death,

Gravestone of William Fee, Lock Pit Cemetery, town of Galen. *Photo by R. Marcin.*

yet the law for that crime alone would not condemn him to the gallows." Regardless of what the autopsy revealed, Fee never denied assaulting the woman; he announced he would force himself on her, even at the cost of life, and then boasted he had accomplished his purpose.

The *Wayne Democratic Press* was practically alone in its contemplation of the fate of the second man in the case and detected no cause for optimism: "Thus Fee died without making any confession, or throwing any light upon the transaction which in the least, can benefit his partner in crime, Muldoon. God avert the terrible death which awaits him."

After languishing in jail at Lyons for more than a year, Muldoon was brought into court on January 31, 1861, and discharged by Judge Knox. The judge gave the prisoner "some wholesome advice" and stated that although his "comrade" had been convicted and executed, he did not think there was sufficient evidence for a conviction. This action "met with general approval," and Muldoon exited the courtroom a free man, amid congratulations from friends.[55]

As for the question of justice served, the newspapers displayed evidence of being plagued by ambiguities as the passing decades granted more room for objectivity. In October 1887, the *Democratic Press*, stating that several men confined in the Wayne County jail swore the south corridor was haunted by a ghost, supposedly that of Fee, gave a brief review of the case and concluded that "a majority of the citizens of Lyons believed him innocent." Fee had occupied the cell on the south side "in which the unwelcome visitor is heard whenever it visits the jail." He had allegedly declared before his execution that he would haunt the place, "and these men firmly believe that he is keeping his promise."

The *Arcadian Weekly Gazette*, in its May 24, 1893 issue, published without comment a statement from attorney Stephen Williams that Fee was convicted on circumstantial evidence and "for his general bad character." Whether Williams held the minority opinion at that time cannot be discerned. After the centennial of the execution had come and gone, columnist Archie Bowler ("Bowler's Alley"), writing in the *Geneva Times* of March 27, 1962, deduced from reading the press reports that "the trial was a mere formality and that the jury's three hour deliberation could just as well have been cut to three minutes." Bowler seemed disturbed by the "Roman holiday" atmosphere surrounding the execution, "with everyone eager to be in on the kill." The editor of the *Democratic Press* omitted words from the trial that "might offend the delicate sensibilities of the readers," but from the number of citizens wild to obtain a seat in the courthouse and a place outside the jail, Bowler opined, "The sensibilities of the people were quite a bit tougher than the good editor wished to believe." The entire episode apparently left him shaking his head in despair over this glimpse of human nature:

> *A strange and sordid tale from beginning to end of an unknown and unidentified woman, alone and friendless in a strange land, turned away from a night's lodging; of her brutal death at the hands of a remorseless killer; of an armed man and boy who heard her screams and didn't interfere because Fee was known to be a dangerous man; of a trial held in a carnival atmosphere; of a verdict of first degree murder based on circumstantial evidence and the testimony of a man who couldn't be bothered to walk around a bend in the road to investigate the victim's screams; and the final, defiant expiation on the gallows amid loud cheers and laughter.*
>
> *So much for the "delicate sensibilities" of the human animal, anno Domini, 1860.*

Chapter 4
ELIZABETH ROGERS AND ELIZABETH BROOKS

Geneva, Ontario County
1870

Afew minutes past midnight on Wednesday, June 22, 1870, twenty-one-year-old Thomas Crouchen of Geneva was on his way home when two men crossed his path near the Methodist church on Washington Street. Robert Mackie, a farm laborer in his thirties, and his co-worker John Cockrall, twenty-three—émigrés from Scotland and England, respectively—had spent the previous three hours making various stops about the city, including a saloon and the Mansion House, where Cockrall indulged in beer and Mackie "the less harmless juice of the apple."[56]

Mackie took hold of Crouchen, asked if he knew where there was a "crib" and received a negative reply. Mackie inquired if he knew where the brick house was on Pulteney Street. Crouchen said yes and proceeded up William Street before Mackie caught him by the shoulder and asked if he could not walk with him. Crouchen said he did not care, although he attempted unsuccessfully to escape. Mackie informed him he had been to this place before, and he was going in if he had to smash the door.

When they reached Pulteney Street, Crouchen pointed out the house and announced he must leave. "No, we want you to go up with us and go in," said Mackie.

"I will walk up as far as Washington Street," Crouchen conceded, "and then I will go up that way and go home."

But Mackie would not release his escort when they had reached their destination. "I want you to go up and go in," he insisted. This time, Crouchen managed to break free and headed toward a nearby house. Mackie did not pursue him and crossed the street with Cockrall as Crouchen watched. The two men approached the residence of Elizabeth "Lizzie" Rogers on the west side of Pulteney Street, south of Washington Street. When they entered the yard, Crouchen also crossed over and stood behind a large tree in front of the house.

Mackie wanted Cockrall to knock, but the latter declined, saying he did not like to knock on people's houses this time of night. Mackie whistled and rapped at the door, which was quickly opened by a tall woman in a white nightdress. She asked who was there, and Mackie identified himself as "John Smith."

"What sent you here?"

"I want to come in," Mackie said, trying to enter the house.

"What brought you here?"

"I have got two bottles of champagne and I want to come in."

"You can't," the woman said, closing the door.

Mackie said through the door that he wanted to treat the girls and was told there were no girls there.

"I saw girls here."

Those girls did not live there, the woman said; they called and went to camp meeting. "There is no one in the house and I am just going to bed."

"Let me come in with you, then. I will give you five dollars."

"I can't do it."

"I am bound to come in."

"You can't; go away."

The men left but were back within five or ten minutes. When they reached the front of the house, Mackie stooped as if to pick up a stone. The woman hurried to the front door and opened it as Mackie was running toward the house. "Don't throw that stone."

"I beg your apologies."

"Don't talk so loud, you will arouse the neighbors."

While Cockrall removed the gate from its hinges, Mackie took a milk pitcher off the gatepost and threatened to smash the windows. "Come here, I want to tell you something," the woman said. Mackie approached her with the pitcher behind him.

The woman seized his sleeve. "Give me that pitcher," she said and took it from him, asking him what he meant. To Cockrall she said, "Put down that gate, what are you doing with it?"

Both men came up to the door, and one asked her for a match. "I have none," she replied. One took a match from his pocket and lit a pipe. His companion felt for his pipe but could not find it. "Will you go away?"

"No, I want to come in."

"You can't."

"I be damned if I don't."

"Please go away, my mother is sick and I cannot let you come in."

"If I have done anything I beg your pardon," Mackie said and started to leave. The men got as far as the gate when Cockrall turned around and asked, "What is your name?"

"Mrs. Rogers. Where do you live?"

"Up beyond Sheldon's."

"Will you go away?"

"No," said Mackie. "I was here before now, and God damn you, I am coming in."

"Please go away."

"I will if you will let me shake hands." Rogers agreed to this and reached out to shake hands with Cockrall. He said good night and walked out of the gate. When she shook hands with Mackie, he squeezed her hand and nearly pulled her out of the door. As they walked out onto the sidewalk, Mackie called back, "We will go, but we will come again."

Rogers set the pitcher back on the gatepost and hung the gate on one hinge. As she locked the door, Elizabeth Brooks, a young resident of the house, said, "I am afraid them drunken fellows will come back."

"Go into your room," Rogers replied, "for if they throw stones they might hurt you." She retired for the night and was just "getting into a doze" when the sound of heavy boots and talking on the street roused her. Next she knew, there was a commotion on the steps.

Rogers carried a light into the hall, set it on the bottom step and looked out the front window to see Mackie rapping on the door and turning the knob. She opened the door and said, "What, are you here again?"

Mackie stood in silence for a moment before repeating his desire to come in. Rogers told him he could not, whereupon he reached through the door and caught hold of her clothes with one hand. He placed the other underneath her clothes and tried to pull them up.

"Now go away from here, God damn you, or I will kill you," she cried, shutting his hand in the door.

"Don't smash my hand."

"Then take your hand out of the door and go away. You can't come in."

Cockrall said he would go, and both went out of the gate and walked on the grass against the fence. While Cockrall leaned against the fence, Mackie went back to rap on the door. Rogers told him again she wanted him to go away. Mackie got his hand in the door and caught her skirt, while Rogers ordered him to leave. "No, I want to come in here," was the only answer he gave.

Rogers stepped into the doorway and pushed him back. She repeated the motion until he was out of the gate. He grabbed her whenever she turned, and she walked partly sideways back to the house. When she attempted to shut the door, either her skirt or his foot was in it. Four or five times she ran him off as he followed her back to the house. The third time she pounded him with her fist but failed in her efforts to strike his face. At one point, Crouchen heard "a sort of thud," and Mackie said, "That's too bad; you hurt my shoulder." She continued to fight him off and with the last blow said, "God damn you, go away and go home, you have fooled around long enough."

She went to push him as she had before, whereupon he raised the pitcher. She caught his arm and then seized the pitcher. He tried to pull her outside, and the two of them tugged at the pitcher until Rogers took possession of it. She struck him with the pitcher again and again, smashing it into fragments. Mackie backed out of the door, which Rogers slammed as he exclaimed, "My God! You have killed me!" Bodily fluids splattered noisily.

Thinking he was vomiting, Rogers opened the door and shone the light on him. When she saw the blood, she pushed the door shut, went to the stairs and called to Brooks, "Come down quick. I have struck a man with a pitcher and he is bleeding."

Brooks handed her a cloak. As she opened the door, Mackie fell to ground outside the gate. Rogers had stepped around his feet and crossed the street when she heard someone approaching on foot. She thought Mackie was coming after her and hurried up Washington Street to the bank, where policemen could always be found. Seeing no one, she called at several other places before receiving a response at the home of Constable William Ringer. A woman raised an upstairs window and told her Mr. Ringer was home but very sick. Rogers asked her to tell Ringer to come to her house; there were two drunken men who had been bothering her for the last half hour, and she had struck one of them. He was bleeding a great deal, and she wanted Ringer to take him away.

When she returned home, Rogers found Mackie lying where he had fallen. She supposed "he was stupefied from whiskey or loss of blood." She threw a pail of water on the stoop and swept up the crockery. After she had finished, she heard footsteps and asked, "Mr. Ringer, is that you?"

"Yes, it's me," Ringer said, walking up to the house. "Here's one man, where is the other?"

"I don't know. I heard somebody run when I came up for you."

Ringer stepped over to Mackie, who lay on his face and side, his feet in the gateway. Supposing the man was drunk, Ringer took hold of him and said, "Wake up, friend." Mackie did not stir. Ringer raised his hand, felt for a pulse and said, "This man's dead."

"My God," cried Rogers, "he can't be dead!"

"*He is.*"

"Go quick and get help."

"I intend to." Ringer left to retrieve Thomas Henson, a blacksmith, to take charge of the body while Ringer notified the coroner.

From the rocking chair in the sitting room, Rogers exclaimed to Brooks, "My God! Can it be the man is dead?"

"Don't feel so bad," Brooks said. "I don't think he's dead; Ringer don't know. Wait till some doctor comes."

Officers came to arrest Rogers at 2:00 a.m. She was allowed to stay home that day to make provisions for the care of her seventy-six-year-old mother, and she and Brooks were placed in the lock-up that night.

A CORONER'S JURY WAS admitted to the house where Mackie's corpse had been conveyed. The body—dressed only in pants, shirt and boots—lay on its back, legs crossed and arms extended. The head was raised a few inches, and blood had congealed on the floor. To the left of the trachea "was a ghastly wound, some four inches long, and penetrating inwardly, a cut that appeared smooth and clean—as one juryman remarked 'as smooth as it could have been done by a surgeon.'"[57] Two slight cuts had barely drawn blood from above the left eye and left cheek. Bruises sustained in the fall marked the right side of the face. The deep gash in the neck had severed the jugular vein, causing death probably within five minutes of the blow.

After the examination of the body, the group adjourned to the office of Justice of the Peace J.E. Bean, where witnesses were examined by Angus McDonald for the people and by former county judge George Dusenberre and a Mr. Pritchett for the defense. "Apparently neither the Coroner nor the jury had anything to do but listen," noted the *Geneva Gazette*. "They asked very few questions, and repeatedly stated that the whole affair was out of the line." The *Gazette* thought the jury could have rendered a verdict if half of the questions were omitted, as so few were to the point.

Rogers and Brooks were brought into court at about 4:00 p.m. The former was described as above average in height and "very spare in frame. She coughed at times violently, as if her lungs might be diseased. She looked haggard and weary and had frequent recourse to her smelling-bottle." According to the *Gazette*, she was said to possess a violent temper and could not control herself when provoked. Some years ago, she had allegedly drawn a deadly weapon on her husband, "Doc" Rogers, "but these are all rumors, and perhaps at this time should not be recounted."

The petite Brooks, whom the *Gazette* reporter found "a very pretty looking girl," appeared reserved and unconcerned about the matter, "except in her sympathy for Rogers. The two are said to be very much attached to each other, having been together two years or more. In the streets where not known, Brooks was to be taken for an honest, industrious young woman, and it seems hard to think otherwise of her."

Elizabeth Hogarth, who lived on Pulteney Street near Rogers, testified to hearing two intoxicated-appearing men talking loudly on the street near the house, asking if there were "any windows we can break." They seemed to be in good humor. She saw Rogers strike Mackie on the shoulder or arm, which he said hurt him, and heard her tell him many times to go away and that she would kill him. After Hogarth shut the window and turned away, she heard something fall and break, which she supposed to be a pitcher of water. A man said, "Oh my God! You have cut my jugular vein." She thought he was feigning this to draw Rogers to the door. "Oh God forgive me what I have done, this night!" the man cried. "Oh! my poor wife!" Rogers's door opened, and in the light Hogarth could see him kneeling on the stoop with his feet off, resting on his hands, blood trickling down. As the door shut, he picked up his cap, got up, took two or three feeble steps out of the gate and collapsed. Hogarth at first suspected he was feigning everything, but his breathing was labored, "like that of a person very near dead."

Physician and surgeon C.H. Carpenter determined from his examination of the body that the cause of death was by a sharp instrument opening the jugular vein. There was no fragment of a pitcher on the table before him that could have produced such a wound; it must, he said, have been inflicted with a narrow-bladed knife.

Lizzie Brooks gave her account of the events leading to Mackie's death, saying she was in her room in the upper back part of the house during this time. The people rested, and Bean informed Brooks it was her privilege to give a statement, not under oath, regarding the affair. She could also offer herself as a witness in the case, which, on consultation, her attorneys decided not to do.

Crouchen said he had heard Rogers threaten to hit Mackie with the pitcher the first time she drove him out. He had not thought Mackie was seriously injured and had gone home after he had seen him fall through the gate.

The final witness, Dr. Jerome Avery, found three wounds on Mackie's body: one over the left temple, and another below the temple, both of which went to the bone; the next began about an inch below and "a little posterior to" the left ear, was about an inch and a quarter deep and had slit the internal jugular vein the entire length, about three and a half inches. He, too, believed the death-wound had been delivered by a thin blade or knife with a blunt back.

The *Geneva Gazette* acknowledged that "nothing of importance was gained" by visiting the scene of Mackie's death other than to satisfy the jurors as to the position of the body but nonetheless shared its gleanings:

> *We had previously examined the pitcher, and found that it was an earthen pitcher, a quarter of an inch thick, and so far as we could see had no sharp edges. In company with the Coroner and the jurors we visited the scene of the tragedy, and noted particularly the places occupied by the witnesses Miss Hogarth and young Crouchen. Neither are more than thirty feet from Rogers' door. There were no limbs or trees or ought else to obstruct the vision of these two persons....There were yet several blood stains upon the stoop, walk, fence and in the gravel paths, where all had not been washed off, there must have been many visitors all day, as the grass plat is considerably trodden down. The spot where the head had lain had been covered with dust, and not yet swept off.*[58]

The jury determined that Mackie appeared to have been "stabbed with some sharp or pointed instrument, in the hands of one Elizabeth Rogers." Counsel for the people claimed murder in the first degree and Rogers's counsel, manslaughter in the third degree. The *Gazette* representative heard only a few of Dusenberre's opening remarks but heard "it spoken of as being given very feelingly. He rehearsed the evidence in all its bearings, plainly and fairly, and in a crowded room, to which all listened with the deepest attention. Mrs. Rogers has very able counsel, who will labor faithfully in her behalf."

Justice Bean committed Rogers for murder, a decision the *Gazette* pronounced "wise and just." On Thursday, June 23, Ringer brought Rogers to the jail in Canandaigua to await the action of the Oyer and Terminer in November. Brooks, in default of bail, was taken to jail to be held as a witness.

As Rogers was preparing to accompany the officer to jail, she requested her next-door neighbor Mrs. Base to take charge of the premises until she knew what was to be done with her. "For I have been committed for murder in the first degree. I did kill the man, with the pitcher; no one else hurt him, but God knows I did it in self-defense. I would give everything I have if it had not occurred."

ON NOVEMBER 22, 1870, District Attorney Hicks moved that Rogers be tried separately, a motion resisted by the defendant's counsel—"or counsels, for Lizzie follows the scripture in employing a multitude of counselors."[59] Present in her behalf were Dusenberre, Pritchett, the Honorable A.P. Laning of Buffalo and the Honorable E.G. Lapham. A "long and spirited discussion" on the subject ensued, the defendants claiming they should be tried separately, and neither could testify in behalf of the other, only in their own defense. If they were tried jointly and the testimony found insufficient to hold Brooks, she should be discharged, which would permit her to testify as a witness for Rogers, thus saving the time and expense of two trials "and better promoting the ends of justice." The court held with the defendant and proceeded to draw the jury. When the panel was complete Wednesday morning, the court reporter and stenographer noted the occasion thusly for the *Gazette*: "*Digression.*—The Court drew a long breath; your correspondent likewise; the Court remarked that made twelve; every body in the court-room said the same thing, it was true." Both sides agreed it was impossible to finish the case before Thanksgiving, and court adjourned until Friday.

COURT CONVENED ON NOVEMBER 25, with Justice Darwin Smith presiding. On a motion from Laning, and without opposition from the district attorney, the court ordered a verdict of "not guilty" in favor of Elizabeth Brooks.

George Nicholas, who employed Mackie on his farm near Geneva, was sworn on behalf of the people. He noted the deceased was a tall man, fully six feet, with a large frame, but not fleshy.

Cockrall minutely described the meanderings throughout Geneva the night of June 21. He had told Mackie that it was time to go home before they imbibed at the Mansion House, but his companion "thought not." Mackie then called on an old friend to announce he was about to leave for the west before they encountered Crouchen. Cockrall acknowledged having consumed beer, but not so much that he didn't know his way home. He had started in that direction after he watched Mackie from the gate at Rogers's house. The last words he had heard Mackie speak were "if he had done anything wrong they must excuse him." He decided to rest awhile when he neared the suburbs of Geneva "and for some unaccountable reason fell asleep." He stayed there until about 5:00 a.m. As for Mackie, Cockrall "gave his opinion that he was in that delectable condition which he expressed as being 'neither sober or drunk'; at any rate 'he had not enough to be a fool.' Did not see him stagger."[60] He had not taken any notice of Rogers's face and could not identify her if he saw her again.

Crouchen detailed his interaction with the deceased from the time they met by the church until he saw him fall in Rogers's yard. "When I heard the crockery smash it seemed as though it came down with tremendous force, either against the building or something that broke it—as though it struck something solid. I did not see the pitcher in anyone's hands that night. It struck something hard, and hard enough to break it."

Elizabeth Hogarth thought Rogers bought the property two years ago last spring and did not know any inmates of the house. Here the people offered to show the house had a reputation of being one of ill fame, to which Rogers's counsel objected. The court held that fact could not be proven unilaterally but "must be drawn from the whole evidence in the case relating to and tending to establish the homicide—the law not permitting the people to attack the reputation of the defendant unless she attempts to prove it to be good."

Hogarth proceeded with her testimony. The loud talking of the men had attracted her attention, and the first words she discerned were something about a gate. She did not think she heard a "connected sentence" of what he said. Rogers spoke in a low tone most of the time, and "a good deal the man said had such a peculiar accent I could not understand him; but occasionally he raised his voice clearly, much louder, and then I could distinguish words." When Rogers struck Mackie, "with a good deal of force apparently," she repeatedly said, "I will kill you—I will kill you, by Jesus Christ." Mackie offered no resistance. At one point, when Rogers was using profanity, he said, "Don't swear so, I hate to hear a woman swear." His tone of voice was good-natured, as it had been when Hogarth heard him ask if there were some windows they could break. She saw nothing in the way of a scuffle between Mackie and Rogers.

Crouchen, recalled, was asked what Mackie said when Rogers was striking him. "I heard Mackie say 'I make no resistance; I am a regular chopping block for you.'"

Ringer said he learned of the homicide the morning of June 22, when he got to the defendant's house. He found fragments of crockery strewn around the door and some on the sidewalk, which he collected and turned over to Dr. H.R. Clarke. Ringer was shown pieces of a heavy brown glazed pitcher, which he judged to be some of what he found that night.

Clarke, one of the county coroners, said he found the body lying on the sidewalk with a pool of blood at the neck. There was blood on the gatepost, and finger marks as if a man had gone out. Clarke raised Mackie's head slightly, and blood gushed out from "a very large" wound in his neck. Between 1:00 a.m. and 2:00 a.m., he made a careful examination with a lantern that revealed blood spattered outside the door and on the side of the house. The step was clean but wet.

Before he gave his lengthy description of the deceased's wounds Saturday morning, Professor John Towler of Geneva Medical College said he had examined the coat that came with the body to see if he could not discover some cut or aperture, "or something with reference to the cause of his death; but I found that the coat had been cut or torn in such a manner that it was almost impossible to make any diagnosis about it." Some parts in front had been torn off and were missing. Two small stereographs and one enlarged photograph of the wounds were produced and shown to the jury, as was a mannequin showing the muscles, arteries and veins in the neck and head. The internal jugular, preserved in spirits, was also presented, but the court did not permit the jurors to examine it.

Over the objection of Rogers's counsel, Towler gave his opinion that it was neither probable nor possible for the wound on the neck to have been caused by any of the pieces of crockery that were then produced in court, but rather must have been the work of a sharp cutting instrument with a narrow blade, "for the reason that the distance between the omo-hyoid and the internal jugular is so very small, and the instrument, whatever it was, passed between them, and had made an incision in the internal jugular and not the omo-hyoid. Whatever there was behind the internal jugular was not injured." Questioned by Laning about other fragments being so broken as to cause such a wound, Towler replied he had not seen the other fragments and would not give an opinion. Again he was asked if it were possible to break a piece of crockery or glassware and leave a piece "so peculiar in shape" as to cause such a wound. "I cannot tell," he replied, "as I have never dissected a pitcher."

Carpenter, recalled and examined by McDonald, echoed the belief that a narrow-bladed, sharp-pointed instrument caused the fatal wound, because "where it went down the second time the wound was too narrow to have taken a wider instrument." The wound was such as to have caused death instantly, "though the man *might* have had strength to arise after being struck; so might a person with the head struck off; but to all intents he is dead, or as good as dead. The person so struck may evince physical signs of life for some time; but as soon as air enters the internal jugular, all signs will end."

On Monday morning, Jane Ringer testified that when Rogers came to her house, she "said she had struck one of [the men], and he was all covered with blood, and she didn't know but she had killed him—she hoped she had." Clarke, recalled, said there "was a bare possibility that such wound could be produced by some pieces of the broken pitcher not produced in Court." A muscle had been cut roughly but not all the way through, "not as if it was done with a blunt instrument, but not with an instrument perfectly sharp." Dr. Avery did not believe the wound could have been caused by any portion of the pitcher produced and thought it "very improbable" that any absent portion of it could have done so. The people rested.

Elizabeth Brooks said she had gone with Rogers to Bethel (now Gorham) to get the latter's elderly mother, who was ill. They arrived home at 9:30 p.m., and Brooks put Rogers's mother to bed. Two young men came in a few minutes after 10:00 p.m., and Rogers took them upstairs to the front room. She told Brooks, "I will go down and close my mother's bed-room door and call you," which she did. The men went downstairs into the sitting room with Brooks and left around 11:30 p.m. Rogers told Brooks she would have to sleep alone that night, and she would attend to her mother. Brooks was getting ready for bed when she heard Mackie at the door. She described what she called "the performance," although she did not go to her window to see it the last two of the four times the men were there. She lay on her bed and did not go downstairs until Rogers called her after the affray. Just before the crash, she heard Rogers say, "Give the pitcher to me."

On cross-examination, Brooks said she was twenty-four years old and had come from Wilkes-Barre, Pennsylvania, where she lived with a distant relative. Mrs. Rogers and she had taken in sewing for men in Geneva, and that was the only means of support she had. "She declined to answer the question as to whether she derived money from any other source."[61]

Rogers took the stand on Tuesday morning. She testified that she was thirty-seven years old and had lived in Geneva about thirteen years. She detailed the trip to and from Bethel and the events at her residence before

Mackie and Cockrell appeared. "Nothing was done" while the two young men were there, "only we talked." She did not know whether the pitcher was broken before she struck or afterward. "I do not know how many times I struck him, for I was afraid of him, and I was frightened. It was all done in an instant."

During her cross-examination, "many interesting items were developed concerning the past life of Mrs. Rogers; she refusing many times to answer questions put, on the ground that it would degrade her. Among other things it appeared she had shot at her husband" and that a bill of divorce was pending.

On re-direct, she explained the shooting affair: "I had been to a circus, and coming home I saw my husband locked arms with the woman he was living with, and he pushed her against me and I struck her; then he struck me and cut my arm with a knife, knocked out one of my teeth, tore off a lava pin, and finally knocked me down. I got a revolver of a man near by and shot at him but did not hit him."

Lapham "eloquently" summed up the case for the defense, "going over the whole ground of testimony, and catching points from the intricacies of the mass of evidence."[62] District Attorney Hicks followed, "and we confess we were surprised by his effort....He, too, went over the whole ground, and at times held the mass of humanity there assemble [*sic*] in breathless attention. He portrayed in glaring colors the crime for which the woman was arraigned....And none hung closer upon his burning words than did the eminent counsel for the defense."[63]

The correspondent of the *Gazette*, who submitted the report before the jury returned its verdict, offered these meditations:

> *Should* [the verdict] *be favorable to* [Rogers] *she will from this affair learn a lesson that will leave a lasting impression upon her mind. Elizabeth Rogers is not without heart; we have often heard of her deeds and acts of kindness, not alone to fallen women, but to some who claim to walk in paths of virtue. Would that she had ever acted in moderation; then poor Mackie would still be alive,—She would not have been arraigned before the world a* murderess.

Long before court convened on Wednesday morning, the steps outside and halls inside the building swarmed with spectators, who upon the opening of the doors rushed in and filled every possible seat and standing space. Judge Smith outlined to the jury the grades of crime, if any, that led to Mackie's death: murder in the first or second degree, manslaughter in several degrees, excusable or justifiable homicide or by accident or misfortune. He briefly outlined the evidence, "stating among other things that the jury would no doubt find that the man was in a state of intoxication, went to the house of the defendant supposing it to be a house of ill fame, supposing he might there resort for the gratification of his passion, and desired access to the house for that purpose."

If the house were of the character Mackie believed it to be, it would be no trespass for him to seek "peaceable access," and he had a right to go in if the door were open to him. But Rogers also had rights at this point. She owned the house and the property, "and it matters not to what use she put it however vile and unworthy it may be." If she did keep a house of ill fame, she had a right to select her own visitants and exclude any man she pleased. She had the same right as anyone else to protect herself against a person coming into her house. By Mackie's attempt to enter her premises and *insisting* on doing so, he was violating her clear legal rights. Rogers had a right to use any degree of force to compel him to go away, "but not such a degree of force that it is disproportionate to the exigencies of the man."[64]

AT ABOUT 5:15 P.M., it was whispered through the courtroom that the jury had agreed. Those "lounging about the halls awaiting the result" gradually filled the room, and about twenty minutes later, Rogers entered with Brooks, "who had continued to remain by her side during the whole trial, and who, it seemed, was bound to cling until the last."[65]

As the jurors entered, "the eyes of the prisoner searchingly scanned the face of each juror as he took his seat as if she would read her doom in his expression. Anxiety—deep, terrible anxiety, was depicted in her countenance as she gazed upon them."

"Gentlemen, have you agreed upon your verdict?" asked the clerk.

"We have," was the foreman's barely audible answer.

"Prisoner, rise."

Rogers stood, "her face pale as death," and fixed her eyes on the jury. The spectators were breathlessly silent.

"Do you find the prisoner at the bar guilty of the murder whereof she stands indicted, or not guilty?"

"NOT GUILTY!"

The foreman spoke "in a calm, clear voice; and as he uttered the words a brightness flashed over the face of the prisoner and lit her countenance with almost a smile, but the expression was one rather of gratitude to the men who had set her free."

As the clerk repeated the verdict, "the court room fairly rung with the stamping of feet, clapping of hands, &c., which the court could not for some time suppress."

Rogers bowed to the court and then to the jurors. Her friends and supporters surrounded her, shaking hands and offering congratulations. After a short time, she retired from the courtroom, "accompanied by a crowd of eager lookers on, anxious to see more closely the face of the woman just acquitted of the dreadful crime of murder."

When the ballot was taken, nine favored acquittal, and one of the three immediately changed his ballot to that of acquittal. A second yielded about an hour later; the third held out until the last moment and after "considerable argument" gave in, "feeling that although he had his opinion and believed in it, he thought of *eleven* men on the other side should be considered better than his own."[66]

Rogers did not plan to return to Geneva but would relocate after visiting relatives in a distant part of the state. She sold the house to village president George Stillwell Conover.

THE *ROCHESTER UNION* DID not see how a jury's verdict could have been otherwise, a judgment the *Geneva Courier* found indisputable. There was "no shadow of evidence," the *Courier* stated on December 7, that Rogers used anything but a pitcher in repelling Mackie from the house. The physicians believed that the wound was caused by some sharp cutting instrument of steel, but that was merely opinion without proof. "The thousands who have been cut by crockery, glass, chips, splinters, stones, &c., and even common printing paper, know that incised wounds are frequently made without keen steel edges."

The *Courier* noted the consistency of the testimony and the expectation that Rogers would be tried for something besides murder, that she would be convicted because she kept a house of ill-repute. One could as well convict a man of forgery because he had committed assault and battery. When the prosecution attempted to introduce testimony as to the character of Rogers's house, Justice Smith "promptly and properly" ruled it out. As the *Union* pointed out, no matter the defendant's character, those at a distance, knowing nothing of the party, must be guided solely by testimony. On that, she was rightfully acquitted.

Chapter 5

HENRY SAYLES

Niles, Cayuga County
1871

After serving an execution in Dutch Hollow, Constable William Dennis rode to his small farmhouse, a mile southeast of North Hope, the evening of Wednesday, May 10, 1871. His horse became ill, and he stopped at a neighbor's, intending to stay the night. Late in the evening, the horse's condition had improved to the extent that Dennis decided to proceed, against the neighbor's wishes.

Arriving home, Dennis remarked to his wife, Maria, that it was a cold night and went out after some tomato plants she feared would be frostbitten. When he brought them in, he asked her if Eliza Jane, wife of their neighbor Henry Sayles, had helped her that day. They retired to their bedroom on the ground floor, leaving their sons and the hired man, Edwin Dodge, in the kitchen.

Dennis was disrobing for bed and conversing with Maria at about midnight when she heard a crash she believed to be an exploding lamp. Dennis sailed away from the bed and fell on his back. Maria remembered that there was no lamp; then the smell of powder reached her through the window's broken glass. She sprang up with a scream and roused the household. When she returned to the bedroom, she found her husband dead. A gun had been fired through the closed window, the charge entering Dennis's right temple and passing out about two inches above the left eye, killing him instantly.

After calling the boys down, Maria told Willie, the eldest, that Pa was dead. She went out to see who had fired the shot, but Willie brought her inside. He went on horseback to the home of Abram Jones, called to him that his pa had been shot through the window and asked him to come over. Willie then rode to notify Sayles, who lived one half to three quarters of a mile away, on New Hope Road. He saw a strip of light at the door but received no answer until he called three or four times. When Sayles finally came to the window, Willie asked him to go to the Dennis house. "My God!" Sayles exclaimed. "Is your pa shot?"

Willie summoned his uncle John Dennis and Dr. William Cooper of Kelloggsville before returning home. As Sayles entered with Mr. and Mrs. Jones, at whose home he had stopped en route, he said, "What! Will shot— shot through the window?" While other neighbors drifted in, Sayles sat in a chair near the stove with his head in his hands. Although he had moved into the neighborhood only the year before, Sayles was well acquainted with the Dennis family, having known William for twenty years and having worked for him and his brothers John and Dwight. He lived in a house owned by Dwight and earlier that day had sown grain for John.

Cooper arrived at the Dennis house between 1:00 a.m. and 2:00 a.m. He found the victim lying face up, still bleeding from a finger-width wound in his shattered skull. His brain was "a pulpy mass."[67] Cooper told John Dennis that someone had to go to Auburn for Dr. Lansing Briggs. Sayles jumped up and said, "I will go to Auburn."

Several buckshot and slugs were found embedded in the ceiling, after passing through Dennis's head. The window, lacking curtains or blinds, bore a powder-burn on its sash, "showing that the assassin was waiting for his victim to enter the house in order to make sure of his aim or ensure his own escape in case of failure."[68]

Around 10:00 a.m. the next day, John Dennis observed tracks extending northeast from the bedroom window for four or five rods toward the fence before heading northwest. They were small and nearly square, made by a shoe or boot with a square toe and heel and scalloped top. The neighboring lot showed tracks where two people had crossed at different places. The next field over was Jones's meadow; the next, a plowed strip, was also marked by small, broad tracks with a scalloped top.

Deputy Sheriff Orisimus Van Etten and Charles Lee examined the tracks and compared the clearest with one of Sayles's boots, which he offered freely. It was a close fit. Sayles told Van Etten he had left the tracks across Jones's ploughed lot going to Dennis's the morning on which the measurements

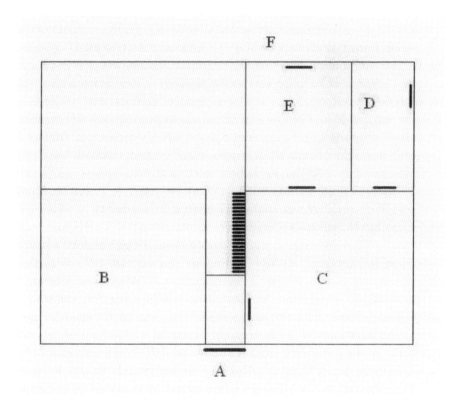

Diagram of Dennis's house. A. Outer door. B. Hall. C. Kitchen. D. Pantry. E. Bedroom where Dennis was shot. F. Windows. *From an illustration in the* Auburn Daily Bulletin, *October 17, 1872.*

were made. These tracks, when compared to those near the house, were exactly the same in size and general appearance. When Van Etten returned the boot, Sayles remarked it was "hard to be suspected."

The tracks in the ploughed strip resembled those from a small boot fitted by Charles Ryan, the only person who could be considered an enemy of the murdered man, as far as anyone knew. Trouble had existed between Ryan and Dennis over a mortgage that caused Dennis to be indicted. Ryan's foot also fit the tracks leading toward Jones's property.

At the first meeting of the coroner's jury, the vote stood eight to four for the arrest of Sayles. After careful sifting of testimony, sufficient evidence was obtained to warrant proceedings against Sayles. On July 6, he was arrested and brought to the Auburn jail to await action of the grand jury in October.

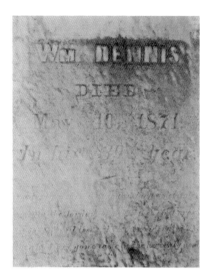

Gravestone of William Dennis, Indian Mound Cemetery, Moravia. *Photo by R. Marcin.*

The trial was postponed repeatedly due to the absence of important witnesses for the prosecution, and according to the *Troy Daily Times*, one of the grand jurors in the case was challenged on the ground that he "had formed and expressed an opinion as to the guilt or innocence of the accused. Judge Foster sustained the challenge, and the juror was set aside. This is the first time in the history of criminal jurisprudence in this state where this question has been raised."[69] By September 1872, the *Auburn Daily Bulletin* lamented, "nearly fifteen months have elapsed, and justice has failed to be done, either to Sayles, innocent or guilty, or to the murderer, whoever he may be."

The trial finally began on Tuesday, October 15, 1872, with the selection of jurors. That morning, a reporter from the *Auburn Daily Bulletin* described Sayles as "apparently about 45," of medium size, weight about 135, dark complexion, black eyes and hair, heavy black beard and mustache. During his confinement, he had been "extremely quiet and well behaved." He had a wife, son and three daughters, the eldest of whom was married.

The monotony characterizing Sayles's life since his incarceration must have been unimaginable, as his elevated spirits on this occasion indicate: "Pleased at the prospect of changing his jail life for other scenes, even though but for his trial, he was apparently in high glee this morning, whistling and dancing as happily as if his life were not at stake upon the evidence so soon to be heard against him." If, as the reporter claimed, it was "thought by many that he is the victim of circumstances, and not guilty of the crime for which he is being tried for his life," Sayles may have believed the outcome would be in accordance with popular opinion.

THE ROOM WAS HALF full when the court opened on October 16, "but the interest in the case soon filled the seats with a deeply attentive audience."[70]

District Attorney Mills discussed motives leading to the crime and promised to show none other than the prisoner possessed them or could have done the act. "The character and disposition of the prisoner was pictured in not very flattering terms."[71] The leading motive, Mills stated, was Sayles's notion that Dennis had "criminal intercourse" with Mrs. Sincerbox, Sayles's married daughter, and also with Sayles's wife. Sayles, under this belief, threatened to take Dennis's life.

Maria Dennis came to the stand dressed in deep mourning. She recounted William's whereabouts the day of his death and detailed the layout of the house. The family consisted of William, herself and four children, ranging in age from three to seventeen years. Her husband had been thirty-nine years old and in good health. She knew Sayles's daughter Caroline, wife of William's employee Charles Sincerbox. Caroline had been at the Dennis residence a number of times, to Sayles's knowledge. William also visited Sayles's home frequently, but Maria did not say why. When he was shot, William had on his person a pistol, which had been in his possession but a short time.

Cross-examined, Maria said that trouble existed over a mortgage between her husband and Ryan, whom she had never seen until Deputy Sheriff Van Etten brought him to the house after the murder. She did not know how long William had carried the pistol or why. Upon his death, it was placed in a drawer. Sayles, who had stayed at the house until the funeral on Sunday and shaved William after his death, told Maria a day or two after the murder that Willie had the pistol and was making threats. He desired that Maria should take it from him.

Dr. Briggs, who examined Dennis on May 11, said he "found [the skull] crushed and brains oozing out, mostly on the left side." The wound contained two or three "battered pieces of lead." He found five in all, which appeared to be buckshot.

John Dennis admitted that he had said he would give $1,000 "to know who did the deed" but denied paying anyone to obtain evidence. The day of the murder, there had been cider in the lot where Sayles worked, but they'd had nothing else to drink and Sayles was not intoxicated when he left.

George Magee, who lived two miles from the deceased, had been directed by the coroner to seize a gun from Ryan on May 11 so that its contents could be analyzed. The gun had not been charged.

Dennis's uncle Thompson Keeler of Moravia had a conversation on May 11, and again two months later, in which Sayles denied having anything to do with the murder. The previous October, Keeler and Dwight Dennis had gone to the jail at the suggestion of Sayles's brother, so that Sayles might tell what he knew. Sayles claimed that he "would have told what he knew about the matter before if it had not been for outside influences."

Dwight Dennis testified that three or four weeks before the murder, Sayles had wanted to borrow money from him; he told Sayles to get it from William. On April 5, 1871, Dwight and William went to Sayles's home to settle an account with a twenty-dollar balance, which was going to Mrs. Sayles. She declined to accept it, wishing William to take it, which he did. Sayles then told William that "things must be changed, or he would beat him in one way if he couldn't in another." William asked him what he meant by a similar remark made the night before. Sayles repeated the statement two or three times in a low, short manner before the brothers departed.

Charles Whiting of Niles related the same conversation of April 5, adding that he had gone to Auburn the day before with William, Sayles and Caroline Sincerbox. At the request of William and Caroline, Whiting was appointed Caroline's guardian in a divorce suit brought by her husband. Sayles had wanted the position for himself but had made no objection until after this *fait accompli*.

John Dennis, recalled, said that Sayles had requested he accompany him to Auburn on April 6, to have someone else appointed Caroline's guardian. On the way home, Sayles repeated his remarks about beating William. On May 1, Sayles told John, "Will had misused him" and thrown him out of employment. Sayles objected to his wife working for William, saying that people were talking about it. Sayles and William had a conversation the same day about breaking a sewing machine; Sayles "said if he knew who told of it he would fix him."

Charles Carpenter described an encounter he'd had with Sayles in April 1871 in which the defendant called William a "big rascal," claimed "they" got him drunk at Auburn and had Whiting appointed Caroline's guardian and said he knew William intended to seduce his wife or daughter. Sayles asked Carpenter if he knew William was his (Carpenter's) enemy; the witness stated he knew Sayles was telling the truth about that.

James Nesbit had heard Sayles say at Pidge's hotel four or six weeks before the murder that he would have to kill or shoot either his wife or himself. Before this, he had heard reports of Sayles threatening William.

Lyman Jones, Sayles's brother-in-law, had been at Sayles's the Christmas before last when he heard Sayles say William Dennis had broken up his family. Sayles took a razor and started out, saying he was going to cut Dennis's throat. Mrs. Sayles went after him and brought him back half an hour later.

Henry Webster, William Dennis and John Jones, son of Sayles's wife's sister, had been riding with Sayles about May 1, 1871. Sayles was sick and told Webster not to tell anyone, or people would think he was drunk, and that he would kill Webster if he did. One day, he said, he would show them something that would make their eyes bug out, and there was one man he would fix. He also had a bone to pick with Webster.

When John Jones lived at Sayles's home four years earlier, he'd kept at the house bullet molds, four or five charges of powder and about half a pound of 3- or 4-shot. When he went back for them on June 9, he could not find them.

In June 1871, at Pidge's, Edwin Dodge told Sayles he could help him if he would reveal what he knew about the killing of Dennis. Sayles tapped him on the shoulder and said, "By God he [Dennis] is out of the way."

Jirah Cady had come to the scene of the homicide Thursday night before dark. Sayles showed him the window through which the shot was fired. He took position where he thought the murderer stood; Sayles said no and assumed a different position, saying that was where the murderer stood.

John Jones, recalled, repeated a conversation he'd overheard at John Dennis's on June 18, 1871, between Sayles and Dennis's mother. "You must be astonished to see me here," Sayles began. She asked why. "Your folks suspect me," he replied. Mrs. Dennis didn't know that they did. Sayles said he had heard afterward they did not. Mrs. Dennis stated they found the gun with which William had been killed, and Sayles asked why they did not arrest him. He accused her of saying they had found the gun at his house, which she denied. Sayles said he would not believe her under oath and asked Jones to leave with him—seven or eight witnesses would swear the murder on Jones, but if he would go home with Sayles, he had the evidence that would clear him. Jones did not comply with Sayles's request, even when Sayles promised to tell him more. As for the missing bullet molds, Sayles claimed that Jones had sold them. Jones, he said, had sworn falsely against him and was the cause of all this "fuss."

The case for the people thus completed, the defense asserted that the prosecution had established no case and moved that the court instruct the jury to discharge Sayles. The district attorney objected that the evidence taken pointed to no one but Sayles. The motion was denied, and court adjourned until October 18.

DAVID MITCHELL OPENED THE case for the defense by affirming his entire belief in the innocence of Sayles, who had "been falsely persecuted by those who have sought his life." He had never known a case of secret assassination committed for the motives assigned by the prosecution; murders for such a cause were always openly committed. He promised that the defense would show that Sayles was home the entire evening of the murder; that the deceased was quarrelsome and had difficulties with many of his neighbors; and that a man was known to have driven from New Hope Road into the pasture lot, to within a few rods of the window, and afterward to drive rapidly away.

Several witnesses testified to the appearance of the wagon tracks across the field, which looked as if they had been made the night of the murder. William Wood, who said he had heard Truman Dewitt call Dennis a rascal and say he'd like to lick him back on July 4, 1870, heard noise as of a buggy going east around midnight that night, and the "wagon was going like the old Harry." Under cross-examination, he stated he'd learned that Dennis went home about the time he heard the noise and that he'd never known anyone to make threats against Dennis. Dewitt was west at the time of the murder and came back in July 1871.

Van Etten, the people's witness, said he found powder, shot and bullet molds at Sayles's on May 11, as well as an old dusty gun that "had not been touched for some time." He did not seize any of these items.

Mrs. Ryan testified she was at Sayles's with his wife and daughter the night of the murder. She arrived before sundown and stayed about an hour. Sayles came home while she was there and announced that he was going to bed. Her husband had gone to "Hope" for a newspaper and came home

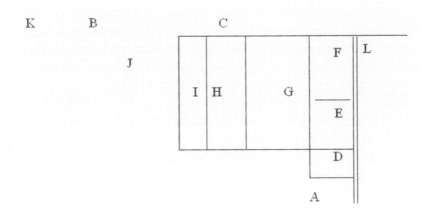

A. Dennis's residence. B. Sayles's residence. C. Abram Jones's residence. D. Plowed field. E. Growing wheat. F./G. Grassland. H. Jones's meadow. I. Plowed strip. J. Gulch. K. New Hope and Skaneateles. L. Lane. *From an illustration in the* Auburn Daily Bulletin, *October 17, 1872.*

MURDER & MAYHEM IN THE FINGER LAKES

soon after she did, around 9:00 p.m. She retired around 11:00 p.m., sleeping in the kitchen, with her husband in the bedroom. She did not wake up and didn't know whether her husband got up that night.

The defendant took the stand during the afternoon session. He gave his age as thirty-eight and said that he was born in Homer, New York. He'd been married twenty years next January. His daughter Caroline would be nineteen on March 27. He'd moved to Niles two years ago last March and had worked extensively for Dennis the first year after he relocated. He acknowledged saying that he would beat Dennis in one way or another. The last time he had seen Dennis was Tuesday night before he was shot; Dennis had come to his house that evening to visit and play euchre. Dennis talked about hiring Mrs. Sayles to work for him the next day, and she agreed. No hard words were exchanged. Dennis left alone around 11:00 p.m.

Sayles stated that he had worked for John and Dwight Dennis the day of the murder, came home shortly after sundown and found Mrs. Ryan there. He was tired and went to bed not long after. Next thing he heard was Willie Dennis calling him, telling him his pa was shot and asking him to come. He had no knowledge of who shot Dennis and had no gun that could be used. He denied remarking that he would have to kill Dennis, his wife or himself. He had made threats against Dennis but never intended to commit personal violence against him, nor had he threatened to kill anyone, at least not when he was sober. He had made no threat in the conversation with Dennis, as reported by Dwight, and had never made any charge against Dennis concerning his wife. After Dennis was killed, he'd tried to commit suicide with a pocketknife when he'd been drinking, but Charles Sincerbox prevented him. He remembered going outside with the razor in December 1870 but could not recall what he said. He didn't recollect the conversation Webster and Jones testified to but didn't deny that he'd had it.

Sayles's fifteen-year-old daughter, Emma, testified to Dennis coming to the house the night before he was killed, as well as to the friendliness of the visit. She'd been home the night of the murder and went to bed at about 9:30 p.m. She woke up, heard her father snoring and went back to sleep until Willie Dennis woke them.

ON OCTOBER 19, JOHN Clark testified that mathematical calculations indicated the man who fired the shot "should have been 6 feet 2 inches high to his shoulder." He didn't know positively the point in the window through which the shot passed. The murderer's height would make a difference whether the shot passed through the upper or lower part of the pane. The shot might have been deflected from Dennis's head to where it was found in the wall. He measured the defendant in the presence of the court and found him five feet, six and a half inches high. The defense rested.

Franklin Lewis, a witness for the defense, was recalled for a rebuttal. He had made an experiment the previous week as to where the murderer must have stood, three feet from the house; he'd placed the gun at his shoulder and aimed it through the window at a shot mark on the ceiling. At five feet, nine inches, he proved to be too tall to get in range. "By measurement it would require a man 5 feet 5 inches." Four other witnesses reported finding no wagon tracks in the field.

Testimony was closed, and court adjourned until October 21.

In his two-hour summary for the defense, Mitchell stated that this was the first time a case had been submitted to a jury on such grounds. No English or American jury ever passed a verdict of death on a man who killed another because that party had ruined his wife or daughter. There was no man who would not, under similar circumstances, make more severe threats than those charged against the prisoner.

If what the prosecution declared was true, Sayles was not guilty by the laws of the land, even if he fired the shot. All authorities show taking life for such provocation was not murder; the law rendered it the lowest degree of manslaughter.

But the jury could not convict except on full proof that Sayles was guilty. A preponderance of evidence was not enough; the proof must be full and conclusive. When it is not clear that no other person could have committed the deed, a jury cannot find a verdict of guilty.

What was the evidence? Sayles said he would "fix" William Dennis if the guardianship of his daughter were not changed. Tracks had been found leading from Dennis's house corresponding to Sayles's boot. Sayles once said that he would kill Dennis, his wife or himself. He had once or twice attempted to commit suicide because of the ruin of his family.

There was not enough evidence, were it all true, to send Sayles even to the state prison. But it was not all true. The character of many witnesses for the prosecution was bad in the extreme, Mitchell postulated, and money had induced the obtaining of much of their testimony.

Nesbit's testimony, that he had heard Sayles say he must either kill Dennis, his wife or himself, was improbable. If Sayles had intended to murder Dennis, he would never have made the threat in the presence of two witnesses. If Nesbit had heard such a threat, he would never have kept it to himself for two months while the country about was ablaze with excitement about the murder. He could not help but speak of it, had it been true.

The foot-track theory was absurd. It was not even pretended that the track was an unusual or peculiar one, but rather was like thousands of others in that region. This sort of evidence was the most unreliable and untrustworthy that could be advanced and could only have weight where the similarity of the tracks and prisoner's boots was proved by peculiar marks and accurate scientific measurement while the tracks were fresh.

The foolish remarks of the prisoner, made while he was "in liquor," were brought up against him. His words after the murder were tortured to contain evidences of guilt, "but there is not a shadow of evidence in these. No one even of us could know, under such exciting circumstances, what he was saying."

There was no other evidence against Sayles. No gun was placed in his hands, and nothing brought him to the scene of the homicide. The jury could not "render a verdict of death on a mere guess."

The defense had shown that a wagon was driven through Dennis's fields to a place near the house and then out and away again—at the hour the murder was committed, no less. Yet the prosecution "endeavored to extirpate our evidence on that point, because they fear that if the wagon tracks are admitted they will show that Dennis himself drove in the fields with the prisoner's wife for improper purposes. But these tracks have been shown to exist; and I say the men that drove that wagon fired the shot that killed William Dennis."

The prosecution asserted that Sayles showed evidence of guilt by appearing conscious of the fact that he was suspected. "But it was natural that he should feel that he was suspected and would be thought the murderer, for he had every reason to feel revenge against the deceased, and had said hard things against him."

This was, Mitchell declared, a case of mere suspicion at worst. There was no evidence that did not admit a doubt. "I believe that this case utterly fails to be proved against the prisoner at the bar, and if what has been said has not been enough to save him, I shall always regret that I did not stand aside and let an abler advocate plead for him."[72]

E.G. Lapham then summed up the case for the prosecution. He called the case "one of the most important that has ever been tried within the borders of this county." The counsel for the defense had no right to charge perjury on the prosecution's witnesses or that one of them could be bought for ten dollars; "such assertions will not do in this intelligent county of Cayuga, though they may in Syracuse."

Had Sayles committed the murder openly, the defense would claim he was not guilty "because he had the motive assigned. This is a monstrous doctrine—this doctrine of temporary insanity, and should not obtain."

The wagon track theory had been invented and magnified from flawed evidence. It appeared from the testimony of Dwight Dennis, Cady and Van Etten that these tracks could not be found. "The theory that these tracks were found, and that the man who drove it fired the fatal shot, does not disprove the theory that the prisoner fired the shot, for he possessed a horse and wagon."

Lapham pointed out the odd circumstances under which Willie Dennis roused Sayles. Sayles had time to go from the scene of the crime to Ryan's barn, replace the gun and return home before the messenger came. Emma Sayles testified that she heard Willie call only once. She could not have slept lightly or she would have heard him each time he called. It was also odd that Sayles reached Jones's before they were dressed, although he had twenty or thirty rods to travel and was called after Jones.

The defense claimed that Dennis had enemies who might have committed the murder but had proved nothing on that point. It noted that if Sayles had intended to carry out his threats, he would not have made them openly. "He would not, if he were as discreet as the learned counsel." Lapham read from the reporter's minutes the various threats and suspicious remarks made by Sayles and argued that they had deep and important meaning.

The character the defense imputed to the prosecution witnesses was an insult to them and to the jurors' intelligence. They were not to throw out or disbelieve Nesbit's testimony because his father died in prison. They had no reason to doubt the witnesses' declarations, and if they were true, they showed Sayles had evil intention against Dennis.

The day after the murder, and thereafter, Sayles repeatedly asked if he was suspected. What could this mean? "The wicked flee when no man pursueth."

The tracks leading away from the window were found to correspond exactly with the boot of Sayles. It was promised that the boot would be brought to the trial, but it was not. Was it not safe for the defense to do so? Sayles called Cady to the north side of the house and showed him where the murderer must have stood. How did he know what the position was?

The cause for grievance assigned to Sayles, the ruin of his daughter, had been resolved before the murder. Caroline and her husband had been reconciled, and Sayles himself said he did not believe the charges of improper conduct toward Dennis. But he showed another motive afterward. He said that Dennis had thrown him out of work, and his wife should not work for Dennis unless he himself did. "Coming home from his day's work, and finding his wife had been at work for Dennis against his remonstrance, he was fired with jealousy."[73]

The *Auburn Daily Bulletin* called Lapham's speech, which occupied slightly less than two hours, "a masterly, logical effort" that "held the closest attention of the audience to its close. The clear manner in which he brought out and welded together the various links in the chain of circumstantial evidence adduced from the testimony, was powerful and worthy of admiration, if not convincing to the jury."[74]

JUDGE E. DARWIN SMITH gave his charge to the jury on October 22. He reviewed the dubious value of the tracks, Sayles's behavior after the murder and his previous threats, stating the case was wanting in many elements that would clearly establish his guilt. The words Sayles dropped after he was suspected were "so liable to be distorted, misrepresented and even manufactured, that it must be accepted with care, if not stricken out altogether." He asked the jury to consider the motive of jealousy or whether the person who drove in the fields near Dennis's house committed the murder.[75]

The jury retired at 10:30 a.m. and returned after about half an hour, announcing that it had unanimously found the defendant "not guilty."

The spectators applauded loudly, and Sayles was discharged. He rose, said, "I wish to return my sincere thanks" and left the courtroom with his friends, a large portion of spectators trailing behind. Friends and strangers took him by the hand and offered congratulations.

"It is wholly superfluous to say that he was in the best of humor over his acquittal and release, after a tedious imprisonment of fifteen months," stated the *Daily Bulletin*, adding that "he hardly seemed to realize his freedom." He made his way to the New York central depot, heading down Genesee Street with his daughter, "whose face bore traces of weeping from the revulsion of feeling caused by his discharge."

AFTER HIS ACQUITTAL, SAYLES "pursued an erratic course."[76] He kept a boardinghouse and saloon in Auburn before relocating to Moravia, where he entered the butchering business.

In early September 1879, residents of Moravia observed that Sayles had been under the influence of alcohol for several days, indulging in frequent sprees. "At such times he would drive his family from the house, threatening their lives and abusing them."

The evening of Friday, September 5, he drove home heavily intoxicated, ran his wife and children out of the house and told his young grandson that he was going to kill himself. The boy informed his father, but as Sayles had frequently made similar declarations, no mind was paid.

Sometime after 7:30 p.m., Sayles's grandson found his warm but lifeless body hanging from a rope in his barn.

Chapter 6
THE FEEDBAG MURDER

Montezuma, Cayuga County
1872

As the *Miles Cleveland* passed through Gere's Lock in the Syracuse suburb of Jedds in May 1872, two young men hailed the canalboat and asked for positions. The twenty-one-year-old Englishman gave his name as Henry Page, and the twenty-seven-year-old Irishman identified himself as Patrick Swain. They had recently arrived from Canada and were great friends, notwithstanding the difference in their nationalities. The boat's owner, Horace "Hod" Exner, made a contract to work with Swain, and Page was allowed to stay on the boat until he found employment. When the boat reached Montezuma, Page secured a berth on the *John Jiffet*.

When Page passed through Montezuma in July, he was offered a position in the day boat barn of Horace Davenport and Henry Stokes, located on the south side of the Erie Canal and west of the Seneca and Cayuga Canal. Page accepted and began his duties at once, taking out teams and collecting money for horsefeed, which he recorded in a book and turned over to his employers. When he had accumulated twenty or thirty dollars, they would take it and leave him about ten dollars to make change. By his regular habits and diligence, Page became a favorite. He seldom left the barn except to take his meals at Davenport's home, and upon finishing, he would return immediately to his station.

An office on the north side of the barn contained Page's sleeping quarters, a money drawer and two bags hanging on the wall. One, black and covered with coal dust, had been brought from a canalboat. Attached to it was a marlin string, or tarred cord, which Stokes had cut in two, leaving a piece about six inches long. The other was an ordinary grain bag with "no peculiar mark on it."[77]

The seven or eight times the *Miles Cleveland* passed through Montezuma that fall, Swain would sleep with Page instead of staying on the boat. "The two seemed warmer friends than ever; in fact, they were almost as affectionate as lovers."[78]

BETWEEN 5:00 A.M. AND 6:00 a.m. on Saturday, October 12, 1872, Davenport found the barn door open and the office locked. There was no sign of Page. He had last seen his employee the evening before, about dusk. After looking for Page for some time, Davenport headed to the barn to milk his cow. Swain approached him on the way and asked if he had seen "his man." When Davenport replied he had not, Swain offered that Page had left the barn last night and said he was going to the village to see his girl. He informed Swain he would not be back for two or three hours and asked him to take care of the barn. Swain gave Davenport the key to the office and a dollar he had collected.

When Davenport and Stokes entered the office, they found money missing from the drawer. By examining the books Page kept, they figured he had about thirty-two dollars in his possession. The two bags had also disappeared.

Inquiry at the residence of Page's fiancée elicited the fact that he spent the evening there and started back around 2:00 a.m. The bed in the office appeared as if it had been occupied the night before.

Predictably, the surmises regarding Page's whereabouts were varied. There was no reasonable cause for his sudden departure or his leaving clandestinely without saying goodbye to anyone. Davenport and Stokes did not believe that Page had taken off with their money but rather had fallen into the canal in the darkness and drowned. The river and canal were dragged for a great distance, unavailingly. It was also feared he had been murdered for the money in his possession, but "no definite suspicion settled on any particular person, and that was dropped, the conviction finally forcing itself upon the minds of the community that he had left the place as he had come, unknown and unheralded, although there was a balance of some $15 wages due from his employer, which it seemed unlikely he would voluntarily lose."[79] With this conclusion, the subject ceased to be a matter of concern.

On August 27, 1873, a fisherman rowing in the Seneca River was struck by an unusually offensive smell. He decided to seek its source, which he was not long in discovering. Lodged in eelgrass on the west side of the stream were the bloated, decomposing remains of what had once been a human being.

The fisherman gave the alarm, and the next day, a party descended on the river. Horace Davenport found the corpse lying face down about a mile and a half from his barn. When he lifted the head with his paddle, he discovered that a bag with the bottom rotted out had been bound around the neck with a cord. Another bag, in a similar condition, was tied to the feet. One bag was new and the other old and black-spotted.

The body was towed to a bridge for examination. The skull was bare, although pieces of flesh clung to the face. As Jacob Shaw drew the body out of the water, he noticed "a red place" over the right eye, an inch and a half long and half an inch wide. The deceased was clad in dark pants, a shirt of green, blue and white gingham, a brownish coat with its single brass button fastened at the top and red and white striped stockings with white twine run through the heels. William Gaston recalled that Henry Page had owned such a coat, and the socks, with the bungling way they had been darned at the heel, resembled some he had seen Page wear. His attention had been called to them one day when Page was walking along the towpath. His shoes had been run over at the heels, and every time he raised his feet Gaston could see the heels of his stockings, which were darned with coarse yarn or twine. Henry Stokes had seen Page running his stockings with white wrapping twine two or three weeks before he disappeared.

As the body had been discovered within the borders of Wayne County, it was brought to Savannah. Coroner S. Weed of Clyde found the head had been nearly severed but could not determine whether this had been done by an instrument or by abrasion of the rope. The deceased had no money on his person. Weed empaneled a jury to view the body, after which it received what the *Rochester Democrat and Chronicle* deemed "a decent burial."

Suspicion immediately attached itself to Swain, who had expressed as much surprise as anyone at Page's disappearance and made no attempt to conceal himself. He had spent part of the summer on the canal, and it was understood he had lately been at Syracuse.

The Galen correspondent of the *Rochester Democrat and Chronicle* offered a vivid speculation on how the crime had been exposed:

> *The supposition now is that the murder was committed near the Montezuma aqueduct, the two bags filled with heavy weights attached to the body and thrown from the aqueduct into the river. Eleven long months have passed, and while the friends of the absent Page, if they thought of him at all, thought of him only as alive and well, his body has been rotting beneath the stagnant waters of the muddy Seneca. Winter covered the unhonored remains with an icy pall which was removed by the warm rains of spring. The hot rays of a summer sun penetrated the placid waters and reaching the body, decomposition commenced. The bags containing the weights that held the body fast in its slimy bed gave way, and it rose to tell the tale of murder, probably committed by the nearest friend of the unfortunate youth.*

Davenport traveled to Syracuse on August 30 to arrest Swain. He encountered the suspect on a canalboat, the first time they had seen each other since the day after Page vanished.

Swain was committed to jail while witnesses for the coroner's inquest were obtained. The next day, he told a *Courier* reporter that the boat on which he had been employed arrived at Montezuma between 7:00 p.m. and 8:00 p.m. the night Page disappeared, and as it was a day boat, the crew stopped to stay overnight. Page wanted to go out and asked Swain to stay in his place at the barn. Swain went to the barn after completing his work, and Page left at about 11:00 p.m., saying that he was going to see his girl. He never saw Page again. Swain "talked freely and without hesitation, saying he was willing to tell all he knew about it. He said he knew no more where Page went than any one else."

Swain was delivered to Montezuma on September 1 for examination. He was held at the Auburn jail for the grand jury, to answer the charge of murder. Adhering to the spirit of fairness, the *Democrat and Chronicle* allowed, "He is, indeed, a fortunate man if he can clear himself on the suspicions that now rest upon him."

SWAIN WAS AMONG THOSE arraigned at the court of Oyer and Terminer on October 8. The large crowd gave way as the prisoners were brought in, "the clank of their chains being the only sound that broke the hush which followed after the bustle of their entrance."[80]

Swain was the last of four prisoners to plead not guilty to murder and asked for court to assign him counsel. The court provided him with M.V. Anstin and George O. Rathbone, Esqs.

ON WEDNESDAY, JANUARY 21, 1874, the district attorney moved the indictment of Swain at the court of Oyer and Terminer, the Honorable C.C. Dwight presiding. After the jurors were empaneled, Horace Davenport opened the testimony for the people.

Henry Page, he said, had been in his employ two or three months before his disappearance. The last time he had seen him alive, the evening of October 11, 1872, he had been wearing new boots and pants and a checked shirt of calico. He customarily wore a faded sack coat with black binding. The day Page disappeared, Davenport had seen him with Swain at the barn; "they were friendly together, as far as I saw."

Stokes's testimony corroborated that of Davenport. On cross-examination, he said had known Page about three months and "had become a good deal attached to him; I have considerable feeling in this matter, have done a good deal to work up this case."

Dr. W.E. Smith of Savannah, who had examined the body, had found no marks on it. Although there was no flesh under the chin, he had discovered no evidence of the throat being cut.

Stokes, recalled, said that two canal drivers were arrested for stealing money from Page. Their guilt was conceded and the matter settled when they paid back the money. He had examined the clothes produced in court, which were similar to what Page wore, "and I should think they were the same." The bags that had been taken from the body resembled the ones hanging in the office.

Horace Exner stated that he knew Henry Page and was at Montezuma at the time he went missing. About sundown on October 11, he put his team in the barn and spent the night with his family on the boat. When he went to bed, he knew nothing of Swain's whereabouts.

Exner observed that when he hired Swain, his employee and Page "were very friendly together, as much so as brothers," and "they seemed to carry their money in common."

A Mrs. McNamara of Montezuma, who lived midway between the village and the aqueducts, remembered being up one night that fall. She went out "to see if my man was coming from the village. I saw two men towing something in the canal. I thought it was a horse; asked them what barn the horse belonged to, they stopped, and made no reply. I went back into the house."

The final witness for the prosecution, Eli Sherman, said that Swain told him Page gave him his boots, but they were too small and he threw them away.

No evidence was offered on behalf of the prisoner. The case was given to the jury at 7:00 p.m. on Thursday, January 22.

Two and a half hours later, the jury announced that it had reached a verdict. After the usual formalities, the foreman stated that they found the prisoner not guilty.

According to the *Auburn Daily Bulletin*, "Swaine [*sic*] evinced lively satisfaction at this unraveling of the rope that hung over him, and retired from court with his counsel—a free man again."

UNLIKE PAGE'S INITIAL DISAPPEARANCE, the circumstances of his murder were not so quickly forgotten. On March 16, 1880, a correspondent of the *New York Times*, writing from Auburn, resurrected some of the county's crimes of the 1870s: "A black, rotted remnant of a feed-bag, and a shoe-knife marked with stains of blood, are curious treasures in a collection of oddities belonging to a resident of this city. Each one has its terrible story, which the collector relates to inquiring visitors with a minuteness of detail that the records of Cayuga County would fail to give; for those stains form a portion of the extraordinary criminal annals of the country, and in their time attracted the notice of the entire country."

Three days later, the *Evening Auburnian* recounted the stories connected to the relics in its front-page item "Cayuga's Awful Crimes." The case known as the "Feed-bag Murder," it said, "was one of the most mysterious tragedies ever known in this state, and its mystery has never been legally solved, although morally its solution is believed to be known." A rumor had circulated the previous summer that Swain had died in a western town and had confessed on his deathbed to being the murderer, but this had never been confirmed.

PERHAPS SWAIN HAD INDEED offered a premature deathbed confession, or word had reached him that Page's murder was once again front-page news. In any case, he returned to Montezuma in July 1880 and, before District

Attorney R.L. Drummond and others, confessed to murdering Henry Page. He implicated Horace Exner, whereupon a warrant was issued for the latter's arrest, and he was confined to the Auburn jail as an accessory to the murder.

Constable Davenport returned to Montezuma with Swain the morning of July 22. Exner was also in Montezuma, under the custody of Constable Charles Humphrey, but allowed "the freedom of the village." He protested his innocence "most solemnly" and appeared "confident that the examination will clear him."[81] According to the *Auburnian*, Exner had "friends who firmly believe in his entire innocence" and suspected that Swain was attempting to shield a third party by fixing the guilt on Exner.

Public opinion did not lean in one direction or the other. According to a dispatch sent to the *Auburnian*, some doubted Swain's sincerity, arguing that by confessing he placed his neck in the halter. (Apparently, they were unaware of the double jeopardy clause of the Fifth Amendment.) Others professed that he implicated Exner for a purpose yet unknown. As far as could be ascertained, no enmity existed between Swain and Exner prior to this revelation. Some villagers believed Swain's story "and that he was induced to unbosom himself by the constant pricking of his conscience, which gave him no peace of mind until he told his startling tale of the bloody crime, which will not be truthfully told to the outside world"[82] until he took the witness stand.

THE AFTERNOON OF JULY 22, Justice Torrey began Exner's examination in the upper story of Shockey's Northern Hotel in Montezuma. Seats ran around the wall of the spacious apartment, which was normally used as a dance hall, and the landlord provided for the numerous spectators by constructing benches with long boards supported by chairs. "The villagers began to assemble long before the hour fixed for the trial and when Torrey arrived the large room where court was to be held was packed to suffocation."[83] Those who could not find seats were obliged to stand, and so dense became the crowd "that the justice, lawyers and reporters were hardly able to perform their labors. They were actually hemmed in by a surging throng of impatient people."[84] District Attorney John Vanderburg of Lyons served as counsel for the defense, facing Drummond.

Swain, in Humphrey's custody, arrived a few minutes before the examination, around 1:30 p.m. Since his acquittal, the *Auburnian* reported, he had followed the canal until 1879, when he was employed at a nursery in Geneva. This season he had labored as a farmhand. Now about thirty-five years of age, he had "the appearance of an illiterate man and the demeanor of a person who has lived a hard life." He had a mustache and a beard of about two weeks' growth, and his features were "bronzed from exposure." He wore a black frock coat, blue checked shirt and blue overalls held in place by a strap. A black slouch hat, "a little worse for the wear," completed his ensemble. He seated himself at the end of the hotel stoop, and a crowd of men immediately surrounded him. "He was as dumb as an oyster, and refrained from conversing with his most intimate friends."[85]

The *Auburnian* underscored the contrasts with Swain in its portrait of Exner:

He is small in stature, has a pleasant looking countenance and possesses a pair of bright eyes. His face was cleanly shaven with the exception of his chin which was covered with a thin growth of hair. He was genteely dressed, and never once betrayed by any outward manifestation his inner feelings regarding the grave crime with which he is charged. His demeanor was unlike that of a man charged with murder, but more like one who felt that he had been deeply wronged, and would be exonerated in the end. His age is about 45 years. He now resides in the town of Galen, Wayne county. Exner was accompanied by his wife, who is a fair looking woman. She was faultlessly, but gaudily attired. Unlike her husband she was an eager listener during the examination. She was perfectly calm and fully believes in Exner's innocence.

Exner's counsel wanted him to keep silent, and although he was not inclined to talk, he told the *Auburnian* reporter he had passed the night of October 11, 1872, on his boat in the village of Montezuma. Swain had stopped in with Page that night and came on the boat at daylight. Exner asked about the team, and Swain told him Page had left the night before to see his girl and had not returned. Swain "did not appear excited and Exner said he noticed nothing peculiar about his conduct." Exner could not account for Swain's accusation—"they were the best of friends so far as he knew." However, in the fall of 1872, Swain was dissatisfied with the amount of money Exner had paid him on a debt. Exner threatened to fire his employee and "understood that Swain intended to whip him."[86]

Henry Stokes was the first witness produced for the people. The last time he had seen Page was at eleven o'clock the night of October 11, 1872, at the boat barn. He learned Page was missing the next day, when he visited the barn between 5:00 a.m. and 6:00 a.m. He described Page as about twenty-one years old, five feet three inches and 170 pounds; his complexion was light, and he had no beard. His recollection of the clothes Page wore the night in question matched those found on the body.

Stokes well remembered the black bag with the marlin string and recognized it in August 1873 when Swain was examined. At the same time, he saw another bag but could not identify it as the other that was missing. Stokes knew Exner; he had been at Stokes's barn the evening of October 12, 1872, where he sheltered his team overnight. The witness had seen Exner in the village the next morning.

On cross-examination, Stokes said the bags had been in the office about one month. He could not say positively that the bags he saw at the examination were the ones that hung in the office. To the best of his knowledge, the bags were missed the day after Page disappeared. Stokes could not remember whether he had testified in Swain's examination before Justice Torrey that he did not miss the bags until several days afterward.

Davenport said he had lived in Montezuma about thirty years and had last seen Page about 6:00 p.m. On October 11, 1872, when they had supper at his house. He recalled Page as about five feet four inches and 155 or 160 pounds. He had sandy hair, natural teeth all in "sound condition," and as far as Davenport remembered he had lost none of them. He had never discovered any peculiar marks on Page's body while he was alive.

Davenport had known Exner eight or ten years and knew Swain slightly. Swain was the first person he had seen at daybreak on October 12, and he'd noticed Exner on the other side of the canal near his boat. When he found the body in the river, the lower jaw was broken at the point of the chin, and he saw a brownish bruise near the right temple. One or two of the teeth were gone.

During cross-examination, Vanderburg drew out that there was nothing peculiar about the clothing or any wounds on the body by which it could be identified as Henry Page. On re-direct, Davenport said, owing to the condition of the corpse, "it precluded all possibility of his positively swearing that it was or was not Henry Page's body."

William Gaston said that the socks on the body's feet resembled those he had seen Page wear but could not swear they were the same.

The *Auburnian* reporter must have found the proceedings less than enthralling, observing that they "dragged slowly along" for the next five hours and reveling in this diversion from the tedium:

> *The atmosphere was stifling until the windows were taken out and a current of fresh air admitted. With the exception of a crying baby,*

which was sent out of the room by the court and an individual who was crazed from copious draughts of strong drink and who insisted upon making a speech, instructing the court and interrogating the witnesses, the assemblage was quite orderly. The drunken fellow became such an intolerable nuisance that he was finally carried out of the court room under the arm of a stalwart constable.

By the time Vanderburg presented his case, the weary reporter could only say that it was "ably conducted" and the line of defense was that the body found in the outlet was not that of Henry Page. Vanderburg had privately told the reporter Swain's story would turn out to be "very 'thin'." The credence Justice Torrey placed in it would determine whether Exner would be discharged or detained for trial.

The *Cayuga County Independent* believed that the location and appearance of the body corroborated the testimony of Swain and left no doubt to its identity, "though some would have the people think it was Pharaoh on his way back from the Red Sea."

At 8:00 A.M. on July 24, the court was again filled with spectators of all ages. Swain's examination occupied the entire session, from the beginning until 4:45 p.m., with the exception of one hour for dinner.

As for Swain, he

made his confession in a subdued manner; he did not appear to display any especial resentment against anybody, although he would arouse up and display a little animation at times under the very severe and caustic cross-examination administered by attorney Vandenberg [sic]....He told his story in his own words and freely....The court room was very warm and the narrator must have felt the effects as well as did the justice, attorneys and reporters, and the constant questioning and cross questioning of him throughout the tedious hours brought weariness, nevertheless in the main his story was a straight one and he did not cross himself but in a few instances.[87]

The *Auburnian* again evoked the atmosphere: Torrey removed his coat and sat in his shirtsleeves, "observing that he meant nothing of a belligerent character thereby." A fretful baby caused some annoyance to the court, and a female spectator became faint and wobbled to the stairway but made her exit safely. "The disturber of the dignity of the court on the previous day" was present but was "beaming with smiles and good nature." The constables occasionally checked the murmur that pervaded the room from time to time but otherwise were not called on. Now and again Vanderburg's questions would provoke a laugh.

Swain said that he lived in Elmira, Chemung County, was single and would be thirty-six years of age the next September. He had known Page about two years and had seen him occasionally at Montezuma in the summer and fall of 1872. Swain and Exner had conversations referencing Page, including his money, of which Swain spoke to Page every time he passed through the village.

After two or three trips, Exner told Swain he wanted Page's money and was going to have it. Exner said he would send word to Montezuma to have a man dress in women's clothes and invite Page to meet him. Swain agreed.

Swain and Exner arrived at Montezuma before dark the evening of October 11. Page had told Swain that he had eighty dollars, and Swain relayed this information to Exner. Swain went to the barn, where he found Page and another canal man. Swain remained in the barn, and about half an hour later, Page went across the canal to get some peanuts. When he returned, Swain was under the impression they were alone. Page left again for about twenty minutes, or until 11:30 p.m. He was gone at least two hours before Swain saw him again, over the towpath bridge, "loading over" to the barn. He was with someone dressed in women's clothes, whom Swain could not identify. "I saw a pair of boots and pants under the dress; a thick black veil over the face…this here party threw a blanket or quilt over Page's head." This was said to be Charles Bogert, who kept a saloon in the village at the time of the murder and had since died of delirium tremens:

I heard Page say Oh! don't smother me!…Exner got up and struck him with a hammer.…Page fell down and laid still when struck. I did not see only one blow, on the head somewhere. Page said nothing after he was struck. Exner then asked me to come and help him take of him.…I went where Page was. Exner and this other party dressed in women's clothes were there when I got there.…Exner reached down and unbuckled the belt, unbuttoning Page's clothes, taking the belt off from around his waist— Exner put the belt in his pocket—I took the gaiters off his feet—I put a stone in each one and threw them into the canal—I then said I would go to the boat and get a bag—I went and got it—I got it from Exner's boat—it was a common grain bag, I used to carry it to the barn to feed the team— when I got back they had another bag there—I do not know where they got it; I did not pay much attention to what kind of bag it was, thought it appeared to be a common grain bag. I could not say much as to its color.

Nothing more was said that I remember before we put Page in the water. When we put him in the water he kicked and moved his feet. We threw the hammer in the water before we did Page....From the time I reached the spot until we put him in the water Page said nothing that I know of. After we put him in the water we put some stones in the bag. I think we all three had a hand in it; then tied a line about his neck, a short line; I think it was the party with women's clothes did that. Next I got a stick seven or eight feet long, maybe ten. Exner and this other party took hold of the rope. We towed him up to the aqueduct, three-quarters of a mile west of here.

When we was going along there was a woman going along on the to-path side. She hollered out and asked if we had a dead horse. I saw the woman; she had a foreign speech. We made no reply. We took him along to the aqueduct, west end, and we drew him out of the canal over the bank. There we tied the bags, one on his feet and one on his neck. The bag I brought off the boat was filled before I brought it off the boat. A little coal and some stones were in it....I tied one bag on his feet and Exner tied the other on his neck. We then put Page in the river, me and Exner and the one in women's clothes. After we put him in there we left him in there right at the west end of the aqueduct, on the timbers...saw nothing of the body after that. Saw no signs of life in Page save the first two or three kicks when we first threw him in the water....I went back to the office. I do not know where they went....

I saw Exner the next morning about daylight. He was on the boat and he hallooed at me and told me to get my team out. He was on one side of the canal and I the other and nothing about the matter was said. Exner told me before we left Montezuma that I had better take all of Page's clothes and bring them on the boat. I told him no, I would not take the clothes but I would take two books he had....I had some money I had collected for teams for Stokes and Davenport....I told him then that I thought I would go and give it to them. He said that if I gave it up I was a fool....Exner said [to a groceryman present] *there was no likelihood of Page ever coming back again for he had the night previous taken the 12 o'clock train to go to England. Nothing more was said in Montezuma concerning this matter.*

Later in the day as we were going up the level between Montezuma and Mud Lock I asked Exner how much he got, and he said $80. He showed me no money at the time. He never did afterwards. Don't recollect of ever having any further conversation with Exner about this subject, that is, not before my trial at Auburn.

Numerous questions about the contents and condition of the bags ensued, and a recess was taken.

When court resumed, Swain returned to the witness stand to outline his biography. He said he had been born four miles outside Kingston, Canada. As a child, he'd moved to Dandas and then spent six years in Hamilton. From there he relocated to Lachine, where he "worked for the queen" in "one of her establishments." At the age of fourteen or fifteen, he was sent to a reformatory for highway robbery. He returned to Hamilton and worked at blacksmithing. In 1861 or 1862, he quit the trade and came to Buffalo, "went on the canal" and remained there all summer. He went back to Hamilton and stayed until the following fall, "did nothing in particular that winter, then went to Kingston for stealing a shawl." His five-year sentence was reduced "because I was a good convict." He left Kingston in February 1872.

At the prison in Kingston, Swain had become acquainted with Page, who was serving a two-year sentence. They came to the States the night Page was

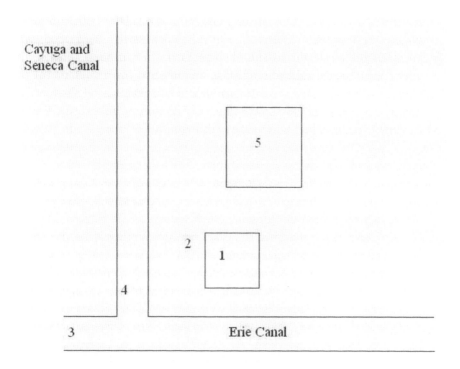

1. Office where Page slept. 2. Where Page was struck with the hammer. 3. Where Page's body was thrown into the canal. 4. Where Exner's boat was docked. 5. Barn. *From an illustration in the* Evening Auburnian, *July 23, 1880.*

released. Swain and Page came west on the towpath to Syracuse and met Exner, who was traveling east.

After Swain and Page separated, they met for the first time during one of Swain's trips to Montezuma in the middle of June. Swain could not remember what they'd talked about except "Canada, England &c." The second time they got together, they discussed money and how much Page was making. Swain said he "was in no way rich"; he was making sixteen dollars per month to Page's twenty. He said that Page voluntarily gave him money several times when he went through Montezuma.

At the time of his arrest in 1873, Swain was on a boat on Seneca Lake. After his acquittal, Swain went to Seneca Falls for two or three years and then to Millport. He had been arrested at Geneva for stealing "old iron," pleaded guilty and spent six months in the penitentiary. A year or two later, he was arrested at Albion for stealing rubber boots and sentenced to the penitentiary for one hundred days; at Canandaigua, he was charged with jumping a freight train and served ten days in jail; he also spent five months in the Buffalo penitentiary for disorderly conduct on the streets. "That is all, and I swear to it."

The *Geneva Gazette* thought many of Swain's details "highly improbable, but as eight years have elapsed since they transpired the witness may have become confused."[88]

McNamara then testified to what she had seen at the canal the night of the murder. The *Evening Auburnian* described her as "a large portly Irish woman" with smoothly combed black hair and dark eyes. "[S]he sat straight in her chair, seemed fearful to press the back of it, and somewhat nervously grasped a black fan and the corner of a small white handkerchief with both hands at the same time…all together her appearance was wholesome and created a good impression."[89]

McNamara said that she had been living halfway between the village of Montezuma and the aqueduct in October 1872. She remembered "the matters of the disappearance of Page" and being out the night this occurred:

> *I walked out a few steps from my house on that night; it looked to be midnight. I saw two men and they seemed to be towing something in the canal. One man had a line in his hand and the other had a stick to keep something off the bank. I spoke and asked which barn those horses belonged to. They did not speak but stood perfectly still. I asked them again and they did not speak. Then I went back into the house. The canal and towpath were between us. I asked them because my husband worked for the state,*

*and when horses died in the barns on the canal, he drew them off....All
I saw was two men. I have lived in that house 18 years and I never saw
anything like that only that night.*

When his cross-examination resumed on July 30, Swain was questioned extensively about how many drinks he had since his arrival in town two weeks earlier but would not swear to any number as he "did not keep any books." He'd had his "mind made up to make a confession all the while."

Dr. Smith recalled the body being brought to Savannah in a slumber wagon. It had been a hot day in August, and the stench was so great that he could not examine the body for more than fifteen or twenty minutes. A center tooth was missing on the left side, and the flesh under the clothes was "good and perfect." He did not notice any particular marks on the body or fractures on the face or head.

On cross-examination, Smith stated if there had been a fracture "I think I would have discovered it....A blow sufficient to produce death would not necessarily produce a fracture of the skull; concussion would be sufficient....A stroke upon the head would not cause the fracture of the jaw as in this case." In his opinion, a body could be kept under water and preserved the length of time this body was. He could not say whether this death was caused by drowning. On re-direct, he claimed that it was almost impossible to determine "without a critical and scientific examination" whether death was caused by a fracture of the skull. "Here the testimony of the witness took a scientific turn," the *Evening Auburnian* inserted parenthetically, "and to give his opinions would be uninteresting and so they are omitted."

After the people rested their case, Vanderburg moved for the prisoner's discharge, speaking for an hour and thirty minutes. "The subject matter was one which enabled him to display himself considerably, and the way he flailed into the character of Swaine [*sic*] as related by himself was enough to make the blood curdle in the veins, and the eyes to bulge out of the sockets of any ordinary mortal, to say nothing of the assembled Montezumians and Justice Torrey."[90]

Drummond held that Swain's confession "had not been shaken by the severe cross-examination by Exner's counsel," and as the justice had given Swain enough credence to issue a warrant for Exner's arrest, the prisoner should be held. If Torrey believed Swain's statements regarding his petty crimes, he should also believe his claims about other people, including Exner.

The district attorney finished around 10:00 p.m., and the matter was turned over to Torrey. "After deliberating about three quarters of a minute during which time he adjusted some writing material that lay before him on the table, he dropped his conclusion like a single rain drop from a cloudy sky, and it possessed no ornamental fringes. It was 'I shall discharge the prisoner.'"[91]

The result surprised but few of the spectators, who extended their congratulations to "Hod," and "there appeared knowing smiles on the faces of many, as if to say, 'I told you so.' The reader will judge from this that there are divisions among the people of Montezuma on the subject, and they expected that this investigation would not change the standing of the matter to any considerable extent, and one might infer from the observations of the actors in the investigation that there were influences at work that were not visible to the eyes of those not familiar with the lay of Montezuma sentiments."[92]

THE *WEEDSPORT CAYUGA CHIEF* reiterated that Vanderburg's cross-examination failed to shake Swain's story in the least, "so far as the main part was concerned." Swain's forced confessions that he had been repeatedly imprisoned for theft and so on created doubts of his credibility, but "of course his character was bad enough according to his own showing, or he would not have been concerned in a murder."[93]

As for Torrey's "extraordinary" decision, jerked out "like the explosion of a pop-gun," the *Cayuga Chief* thought the community had a right to demand an explanation:

> *What is his theory of the case? Who perpetrated this crime, and shall the guilty escape punishment?*
>
> *The object of the examination before a Justice of the Peace is merely to ascertain whether there is sufficient evidence to warrant a judicial inquiry according to the forms of law. The registrar is not expected to pass upon the guilt or innocence of the accused. He has no power to do so, for murder or manslaughter is beyond his jurisdiction. But the discharge of the prisoner is tantamount to saying that there is no suspicion against him. By what process of reasoning this modern Dogberry came to that conclusion, is what the public would like to know. Perhaps Mr. Torrey has ascertained that Page was never killed at all or that no body was found near the aqueduct. The proceedings before him smack too much of the kind of justice they dispense in Texas to be exacted in the county of Cayuga.*

The *Syracuse Standard* had no objection to this denouement, although it may have lamented the outcome for Swain: "The thing is clear. Swayne [*sic*] is a bloodthirsty Hibernian who committed a murder for the sake of Page's money. His conscience hurt him so that it lead him to confess his crime; but he hadn't 'sand' to bear the penalty for his misdeeds like a man, so he put up a job with the McNamara woman, and then declared that Exner was accessory to the murder. Justice seems, in this case, to mean justice, for a change."[94]

Chapter 7

RICHARD BARBER

Ulysses, Tompkins County
1888

R ichard and Ann Mason, both in their seventies, occupied "a comfortable dwelling" on their thirteen-acre farm two miles south of the village of Trumansburg. Richard, known as "Dicky," was characterized in the *Ithaca Daily Journal* as "an inoffensive, kind-hearted man" who had always been hardworking and honest.

Around 10:00 p.m. Friday, March 16, 1888, two of their neighbors, Milton Cuffman and Fred Woodin, discovered the Masons' house in flames. They ran to the fire and found the nearly insensible Richard Mason lying in the snow in his orchard, his hair and clothing saturated with blood.

When Mason roused, the neighbors asked him who had done this. "Dick Barber did it," he replied. He pointed to the burning building and implored them to get his wife out. Cuffman and Woodin ran to the side of the house where the bedroom was located and broke a window, but "the interior was a seething mass of flame and no attempt to rescue anyone within was possible."[95] They carried the wounded man to the residence of Orrin Clark, while the light of the blaze sent residents of the vicinity hurrying to the scene.

One of these was William Allen, who was on his way home from Trumansburg. He was "told the condition of affairs," whereupon he drove back to Trumansburg, informed Dr. Flickinger, the coroner, and headed back to the fire. He was about a mile south of Trumansburg when he saw a man leap over a fence in front of him. Suspicious of this individual's activities in a field in the middle of the night, he overtook the man and asked him to ride with him. Allen recognized Barber immediately and engaged him in conversation about farm labor and such as he drove through town to John Van Auken's barn. Fearing that he might lose his man, Allen proposed to put out his horse and go to a dance. He asked Barber to get out and open the door so that he could drive in. Barber had partly accomplished this when he turned and ran down the street.

Van Auken and Constable Williams were in the barn awaiting the return of someone who had gone to the fire, "and John, tho' not built for speed, took after the runaway"[96] and caught him. When he grabbed Barber and told him he wanted him, Barber's only response was "all right."

On the way back to the stable, an enraged crowd descended on the suspect.

"Damn him, hang him!"

"Damn him, kill him!"

"You son of a bitch, what did you do it for?"

Barber remained calm as the shouting mob trailed them back to the stable. Van Auken turned Barber over to Williams and sent for Undersheriff Edwin Bouton, who arrived amid rough speech directed at Barber and threats to throw him into the fire. Van Auken shook his fist at Barber, at which he appeared nervous. After searching Barber, Bouton handcuffed the objecting suspect, loaded him into a sleigh and took him to Orrin Clark's.

As Bouton placed Barber before Mason, Flickinger, who was tending to the victim, said, "Dicky, look up and see if you recognize this man."

Mason partly raised himself, turned his battered face to Barber and cried, "You villain! Why did you beat me thus, burn my house and my poor wife in it? Why did you do it? You villain, you villain," and sank back exhausted.

Barber's arm shook as if he were anxious, but he said nothing. "God damn you, why don't you answer him?" Van Auken demanded. Barber replied that he did not remember doing it.

When he had recovered sufficiently to speak of his ordeal, Mason said he had been at his barn attending to his cows and returned to the house around 9:00 p.m., when he met Barber near the back door. Barber and the Masons had been "the best of friends"; he had brought them presents and would come to the house and play the accordion for Ann, who was fond of music. Mason invited him in.

They had a friendly visit for about an hour, during which they ate apples and Mason asked Barber to stay all night. Barber didn't think he would.

Mason went into the basement for more apples and passed them to Barber. Realizing that the one he had given his guest was not good, he went to get another when Barber struck him over the head with some kind of instrument. He asked Barber why he struck him, and Barber responded by knocking him to the floor. Barber entered an adjoining bedroom where Ann slept and, as her husband lay helpless, dealt her several blows, which Mason heard distinctly along with her groans. Barber kept it up until the groaning stopped and he supposed she was dead.

When Barber came out, Mason asked him why he did this. "What do you want to kill us old folks for? It isn't property you want?" Barber did not reply but proceeded to pound Mason, making his head, in the words of the *Journal*, "a complete checkerboard." Mason begged him to stop and go away, but Barber ignored his pleas. At intervals, he would open the front door, as if scouting the premises. Mason crawled under the table and asked Barber to go into the bedroom and see his wife. Barber attempted to pull Mason out from beneath the table, but he did not exert much effort; Mason held on to the table and resisted. He asked Barber again to take a lamp and go into the bedroom and he would follow, hoping he could get his revolver while Barber was out of the room. Barber watched his victim for a while but did not leave.

Mason asked Barber to close the front door, as his feet were cold. Barber covered Mason's feet with a mat, papers and other objects, took a lamp from the table, poured the oil over the pile and set it on fire. He fired articles on another table by placing two lamps together, one of which exploded. He went out to the stoop and watched the fire through the partly opened door awhile before shutting it.

The lower portion of Mason's body had become covered with a loose garment, which he managed to kick off as it burned. Rolling and crawling on his knees, blinded by smoke and blood flowing from a dozen wounds, he reached the door leading to the yard. The cold air revived him somewhat, and he crawled to a woodpile, where he hid himself, fearing that Barber would return and kill him outright.

A reporter from the *Trumansburg Free Press* who entered Clark's house found "a most horrible sight": Mason, groaning and covered with blankets, lay on the floor. "His face and head presented a gory mass with hardly a feature distinguishable, his hair a mass of clotted blood, little pools of which had also formed on the floor where he lay."

When Bouton went to see Mason, the coroner was dressing his wounds and "there were cuts on his head four inches long that you could lay your finger into."[97] The length of the cuts totaled more than forty-one inches.

Richard Mason. *From the Ithaca Daily Journal, March 19, 1888.*

AFTER TAKING BARBER TO face his victim, Bouton brought him to Trumansburg and placed him in the engine house overnight for safekeeping. Bouton said that he had "no little difficulty" in preventing the people of Trumansburg from lynching the prisoner, and there were frequent cries of "get a rope, hang the — — — —," and so on. The next morning, with his right wrist handcuffed to Bouton's left, Barber was led across the platform to a waiting bus bound for Ithaca.

An *Ithaca Daily Journal* reporter who studied the prisoner's face en route found nothing "to indicate a desperate character." In reply to questions, he said he was twenty-seven years old and had lived near Trumansburg about eight years. "Questioned relative to the crime with which he is accused Barber would make no reply."

"He seemed greatly agitated and during his ride from the depot to the jail, the muscles in his face twitched constantly and his eyes denoted the emotion which he felt. It was evident he had not recovered from the trial to his nerves occasioned by the mob's threats while he was in Trumansburg." Barber was described as about five feet, nine inches in height, with a complexion "that is a cross between fair and dark." He had a light-brown mustache and was neatly dressed in a dark suit and brown overcoat. His build was muscular, and he bore "the appearance of a man of good habits."

When a reporter asked Bouton the motive of the crime, the undersheriff replied, "Well, that is hard to get at, but a reasonable theory is that robbery was at the bottom of the affair. Barber knew that the old people had about $100 in the house, and it may be that he went there for the purpose of getting that, but in his excitement after assaulting Mr. and Mrs. Mason he left without taking anything."

A woman on the bus who knew Barber "addressed him pleasantly," whereby he "broke down completely and cried for several minutes." After that, others tried to draw him into conversation, but he said nothing.

To a reporter who called at the jail Saturday afternoon, Barber stated that he was born in Lincolnshire, England, and had come to America about eight years ago with his aunt. Nearly all that time he had lived near Trumansburg. The Masons, no relations of his, lived three miles from him. When asked his father's first name, he said, "Am I obliged to answer that question?"

"No, sir, not unless you want to. If there is anything you want to say in your own behalf you have the opportunity now. This is a serious thing and we don't want to put you in any false position."

Barber said he had not retained counsel but would like to send word to attorney David Dean. The reporter promised to do so. Barber said he had never been arrested before and was not a drinking man. His father, around fifty-five years of age, was a farmer, and Barber heard from him about once a month.

"This will not be very good news for him?" asked the reporter.

"Not very good."

To a man who accompanied the *Journal* representative to the jail, another inmate said that Barber "admitted that he killed the old lady, but he said he didn't know how he happened to do it."

Barber turned away after his interview "and sitting on the edge of the table in the centre of the big iron cage lighted a cigar and proceeded to narcotize his shaken nerves." A one-armed inmate proposed a game of checkers with Barber, and when the reporter left, the accused murderer was absorbed in the game.

The *Free Press* found Barber "not bad or vicious looking" and apparently "indifferent to what disposition will be made of him." He "recognized acquaintances with a smile, and when looking in his stolid, expressionless face, we ask ourselves, is it possible that that man can be so indifferent after being five hours in hell, for his heart must be that."

The motives for the crime were not yet developed, but one theory was that although Mason was seventy-four years old, he was likely to live much longer, and Barber, who considered himself next of kin to the Masons, became impatient for the property and resolved to make himself the heir at once. There was no evidence of a quarrel, for when Mason received the first blow he was offering apples to his guest. "What an ungrateful wretch this must be to so abuse generous hospitality."[98]

As for the money the Masons kept in a tin can in the pantry, it could not be found in the debris of the house, which had burned to the ground. The money was not found on Barber's person, but as Flickinger pointed out, "That of course would be no evidence that he did not take the money."

Remains of the Mason house. *From the* Ithaca Daily Journal, *March 19, 1888.*

Richard Barber. *From the* Ithaca Daily Journal, *March 17, 1888.*

On Saturday, March 18, Flickinger empaneled a jury that, after hearing Mason's testimony, rendered a verdict that Ann Mason came to her death at the hands of Richard Barber. Her remains had been taken out of the ruins that day and delivered to the undertaker for interment. All that remained were the head and trunk without limbs, as well as a few bones.

Frank Morse, a petty offender who was discharged from the county jail that day, told the *Journal* that he'd overheard a conversation between the inmates of the general cell shortly after Barber was ushered in Saturday.

"Hello!" one of the prisoners greeted Barber. "What are you in for?"

Barber smiled slightly and said, "Oh, nothing much."

Someone else in the group repeated the question, and Barber replied he was "in for murder and arson."

"Are you guilty?" asked Morse.

"They say I am, but I don't remember anything about it."

A photographer took Barber's picture for the *Journal*, from which an artist made a cut for Saturday's edition. Barber did not want his picture taken and shifted his face to blur and prevent a clear negative.

"Curiosity, that most peculiar trait, is giving Sheriff Follett abundant occupation exhibiting the interior of the county jail since Barber's incarceration," the *Journal* announced on Sunday, March 19. "Of course the accused murderer in the cage is the real magnet which attracted fifty persons or more yesterday and a greater number Friday and to-day." The *Journal* reporter was admitted to the barred general corridor Saturday evening:

> *Some ordinary, petty offenders who would struggle to remain rather than escape were grouped about a long table in shirt sleeves and stockinged feet. A cigar box filled with cheap smoking tobacco and a dozen or more story weeklies and illustrated papers lay on the table....*
>
> *"Where is Barber?" demanded the sheriff.*
>
> *"In his cell sir, lying down," responded an obliging thirty day imbiber of fire water.*
>
> *"Ask him to come out here few moments," was the request which caused Barber a few moments later to emerge to the door of his dungeon. He did not come out into the room but stood in the narrow entrance of the half opened door of bolted bars furnishing him a partial screen.*
>
> *"Barber," said the sheriff, "these gentlemen have come to call upon you."*
>
> *Slowly the young man raised his eyes, looked at the faces before him in a listless, uninterested way, and let them drop again. His visitors, with the sheriff, having looked upon the young man whose name and deeds are now*

executed throughout the whole county, withdrew to a distant portion of the room leaving the JOURNAL reporter alone near him. He has not a face or head suggesting anything cruel or abhorrent. On the contrary, he impresses one rather pleasantly....His face is impassive but intelligent. He seems to thoroughly understand and control himself. There was not the tremor of an eyelid, the quiver of a muscle nor the slightest emotion manifested in the reporter's half hour interview with him. It is a matter of genuine surprise whether innocent or guilty that any man at the dawn of life can maintain such perfect composure and indifference under such terrible charges.

Barber said that no friends had been in to see him and that he had no relatives of means who would assist him. He still had not secured a lawyer and did not answer the question whether he had money to retain one.

Barber had not seen the weekend newspapers and asked what they said. The reporter promised to send them to him the next day. He asked what the reporter from the *Journal* who was there the day before had said about him and was assured that he had been treated fairly.

The reporter could not tell him how much it would cost to hire a lawyer, but the more competent a lawyer he had the more it would cost him; he needed the best money could hire if he wanted to fight for freedom. Perhaps it would cost him $500 or $1,000. Barber had written a letter to a Mr. Donahue, asking him to send his clothes by Bouton, who was to come down Tuesday. He had left the letter unsealed, as he supposed the sheriff had to read it before it was sent.

"Speaking of Deputy Bouton, he had some fears that he would be unable to get you safely away from Trumansburg and on the train to Ithaca. Were you afraid of being mobbed?"

"No. They were mostly boys who followed us to the depot. There was quite a crowd in front of the engine house."

Upon being told that the other *Journal* man had conveyed his message to Dean, Barber asked, "I wonder why he don't come then?" Barber didn't know him but happened to hear him trying a rape case in court three years earlier when he was taking out his naturalization papers. He didn't know if he was defending or prosecuting, but "they were trying to get $300 blackmail out of a fellow as near as I could understand it and I think Mr. Dean got the man clear." David Dean was, in fact, the former district attorney who would represent the people in Barber's trial, due to the illness of District Attorney Clarence Smith.

By Tuesday, more elements of Barber's past had surfaced. He was spoken of as a man who never shirked his tasks but was not well liked by his fellow laborers because of his "reserved, stolid manner." He had worked at one time for Stephen Paddock, at Pine Ridge near Waterburg. It was said in that neighborhood that Paddock hauled out some straw to be ploughed under, whereupon Barber, who did not like the idea, touched a match to it. Paddock, understandably "provoked," discharged Barber immediately.[99]

Thomas Donahue of Trumansburg, for whom Barber worked at the time of the murder, was in town Monday seeking to retain a lawyer for his "unfortunate employe" and was reported to have said he could not believe that Barber was guilty of the crimes charged against him.[100]

A.A. Hungerford was designated Barber's counsel, with assistance from George Davis. The *Journal* stated that it was the general feeling that a plea of emotional insanity would be adopted in defense.

Barber's trial opened on October 16, with Judge Walter Smith presiding. The *Journal* of October 17 observed that the public had so far shown very little interest in the case. Only a few spectators were in court the day before, when the jurors were empaneled.

Clarence Smith testified that he had seen Richard Barber Saturday last and the day before, "and observing his talk, conduct and appearance and judging from that I should say he was *insane*." Despite the defense counsel's objection, he read Mason's narrative of the events of March 16.

Flickinger expressed his belief that Mason was struck with a piece of wood. All fourteen of his wounds were on the head, and although the skull was not fractured, the bone was laid bare on top. Several witnesses described the path of size seven tracks in the snow pointing toward the Mason house.

"Barber," according to the *Journal*, "appears as cool and unconcerned as any man in the room. At the close of yesterday's proceedings he was surrounded by a curious and admiring crowd, composed largely of ladies. He bore the curious gaze of the audience, and listened to their audible comments with the same stolid composure that has so far characterized him. He seems somewhat interested in the proceedings and a smile occasionally flits across his stoical features at the amusing bull of some excited witness."[101]

The courtroom, which had been crowded the previous afternoon, appeared deserted the morning of October 18. Clarence Smith announced that the people were ready to rest. Hungerford expressed surprise at the early closing of the people's case and stated that he was not prepared to open for the defendant that morning. The court adjourned until 2:00 p.m.

At 2:15 p.m., Hungerford commenced his opening. A peculiar form of insanity, he claimed, had existed in the defendant's family from his grandfather down, known as epilepsy. The young man, with "his life of weary days and restless nights," had labored under disabilities his entire life and was of good character. The *Journal* emphasized that Hungerford and Davis had prepared the "most elaborate defense at a great outlay of time and expense to themselves.…The prisoner and his friends being poor people, necessitates the personal responsibility of the counsel for a large outlay of money, with no prospect of reimbursement or reward; unless it be, possibly, an approving conscience."

Davis read several depositions by witnesses from England, beginning with Thomas Blasson of Billingsboro, a surgeon and medical practitioner. He had known Barber from his birth and attended him more than forty times for epileptic fits. During these attacks, and for a short time after, he observed "delirium and violence" in Barber. All of Barber's relatives were affected by severe epileptic seizures: his aunt Ann Johnson was rendered insane by them; his great-uncle William Johnson drowned in a ditch during such an attack; the witness had treated Barber's cousins, grandfather and siblings for the affliction. When Barber lived in Billingsboro, the witness knew him as a "most well-behaved lad," quiet, steady and generally respected. He was not robust and sometimes had severe pains in his head.

Barber's mother, forty-nine-year-old Sarah Barber, stated that all of her nine children had been subject to fits. Two of her daughters died thus, and as a child, Richard had fits almost weekly, sometimes several in one week. He was always "very violent" during these attacks and had to be restrained to prevent him from injuring himself or others. The most violent parts would last fifteen to twenty minutes, the entire attack an hour and a half. He had more than four hundred of these before he was nine years old. Richard was "of a good-natured, pleasant disposition and very kind hearted; he was a good, attentive, affectionate son and brother; he was temperate and steady, a regular attendant at church, and a steady and industrious workman."

Mrs. Donahue, wife of Barber's former employer, testified that the defendant suffered from a severe skin affliction that left his bed sheets "very badly mussed and bloody." He often complained that he could not sleep well and would not drink tea or coffee because it gave him a headache.

Barber's aunt, Mary Harmston of Trumansburg, listed the relatives who suffered from fits but said she never saw Richard have any.

Witnesses who had known Barber from his employment at Peach Orchard on Seneca Lake testified to his gentlemanly behavior, neatness and industriousness. He had complained of pain in his eyes, once claiming to be blind for a day, and his hands were badly cracked.

Robert Hugman, keeper of the jail, said that Barber was "usually kind and pleasant," except one time when he came at him with a privy cover. His health had not been good lately, and sometimes he looked haggard and forlorn or acted downhearted.

Professor Sanborn, who had observed fifty thousand insane patients in twenty-five years, did not think that Barber had a vicious face, but the first thing that attracted him was his "singular epileptic eye." He had examined him at the jail and concluded that he was an epileptic. In his opinion, at the time Barber committed the crime he was in a condition known to the medical world as "epileptic fury."

A string of physicians supported this view, citing the loss of memory and confusion often following epileptic attacks. Dr. Henry Allison of the Willard Asylum stated, "Epileptics often perform acts apparently of premeditation; sometimes epileptics know the act to be wrong, but are unable to refrain from the commission of it, at others the mind is so confused that I do not think they are aware of doing any act."

Dr. Robert Morris believed that the crime was committed in an outburst of Larvated epilepsy, which "may show itself in foolish acts, or the most relentless and brutal form of homicidal mania." He did not think that Barber's effort to escape was inconsistent with epileptic furore.

According to Dr. John Kirkendall, "the peculiar manner in which the act was done is evidence of epilepsy; also the general look of indifference; his standing in the road and talking with an acquaintance, riding with him and disclaiming any knowledge of the origin of the fire, remaining all the time perfectly cool and unconcerned, would be an evidence…of a continuing dazed condition of the mind." Another Ithaca physician, J.A. Lewis, said, "A sane man would not kill an old man in cold blood as described in this case."

Several rebuttal witnesses who had known the Barber family in England claimed that they had never seen anything unusual about the defendant. More acquaintances of Barber gave testimony in a similar vein on Saturday and Monday, and other physicians echoed the testimony of their colleagues. The final witness for the defense, Ithaca shoe merchant Patrick Wall, said that he had measured Barber's foot, shoe and rubber, yielding respective measurements of 8, 9 and 9½. "The difference in size between seven and eight and eight and nine would be one-half an inch."

Dr. Ford of Utica, sworn on Tuesday, said that he had examined Barber and found "no condition other than a healthy normal man." All signs pointed to his sanity at the time of the murder: nineteen years of good health and absence of "mental derangement," his consciousness, fleeing the scene, looking up and down the road with the door knob in his hand. His calmness and composure were inconsistent with an epileptic furore, and Ford did not believe that Barber was an epileptic or ever had been. On the question of heredity, there was no evidence except Barber's own statement.

Barber's actions after the murder and his conversation with Allen led Dr. Eugene Baker of Ithaca to believe that he showed sanity and a recollection of what he had done. His apparent coolness and deliberation were strong factors—an insane person would not be more likely to strike when the eye of his victim was turned from him. In an attack of epileptic mania, a person would strike out regardless of the position of his victim. Lighting a fire with a match would also be inconsistent with the theory of epileptic furore.

DAVIS SPENT FOUR HOURS summarizing the case for the defense the afternoon of October 24 and spoke for an hour and a half in the evening. "As an oratorical effort it was superb," noted the *Ithaca Journal*, "and the close attention with which his able and logical remarks were received, evinced the interest the counsel had aroused in the audience." He reviewed the law as applicable to the case, the disability under which counsel for the defense labored and the evidence produced on both sides.

Dean began his summary for the people the morning of October 25. The theories of the so-called experts regarding evidence of epilepsy in the defendant furnished the only plausible or reasonable plea "that up to that time had suggested itself to their minds":

The expert, who, alone of all mankind, discovered the defendant in an attack of petit mal in the jail, characterized his vacant stare as like that of Lady Macbeth; did Lady Macbeth ever display such vacant stare until she was accessory to the murder of Duncan? The body of a murderer is the coffin of a dead soul, and the eye of the murderer glazes into stoniness before the clear glance of purity and innocence. Too far fetched is the theory of the experts that this man put a candle into his pocket and walked three miles to have an epileptic fit in the secluded home of some aged and defenseless couple, resulting in the death of one and the insanity of these two old people.[102]

It was in evidence that Barber piled combustible material on Mason, deliberately poured lamp oil on it, drew a match from his pocket and set fire to the whole. "What a wonderful display of an *epileptic furore*!…How peculiar that this man should show much ingenuity in his different acts to complete the hellish work he had begun. A great thing is epileptic insanity for criminals and murderers!"

It was said that Barber had no motive. What became of the few pieces of silver that were in the house? "Did not Judas betray his master to the Sanhedrim, and become accessory to that greatest of all murderers, for a few pieces of silver?"

Dean closed his "eloquent and earnest plea"[103] at 12:45 p.m., and the court took a recess.

BEFORE COURT OPENED IN the afternoon, every available foot of space in the room and gallery was occupied, and crowds filled the lower halls and even the courthouse grounds. The trial was the sole topic of conversation, "and speculations were rife as to what the verdict of the jury would be."[104]

Judge Smith informed the jury that if the defendant killed Ann Mason while committing the crime of arson in the first degree—burning a house in which there was a human being at night—he was guilty of murder in the first degree. If the victim's death was caused by the defendant's blows, or the fire set, and they found him responsible for his acts, their verdict would be guilty in either case. He was not guilty by reason of insanity if he had no knowledge of his acts and the consequences.

At 9:00 a.m. on October 26, the jury found Barber guilty of arson in the first degree. Smith informed them that they could not return such a verdict. If Barber were guilty, it must be for murder in the first or second degree. Arson had nothing to do with the jury's deliberations, unless they found that Barber killed Ann Mason while in the act of committing arson in the first degree. The jury retired to revise its verdict. At 9:30 a.m., the foreman announced that they had found Barber guilty of murder in the first degree.

Barber received the verdict "with the same stolid composure and utter lack of feeling, which has characterized him throughout the trial."[105] However, one of the witnesses found Barber crying bitterly that day. She asked him why he killed Mrs. Mason, to which he replied, "I don't know any more about that crime than the dead in the grave." On October 27, the *Journal* reported that his demeanor had been "characterized by hopelessness and resignation." He had told Davis, "I am sorry for two things. I am sorry for my mother and I am sorry that I shall not be able to pay you for what you have done for me." Davis tried to encourage him, "but his words did not seem to lighten the prisoner's despondency."

In an interview with a reporter, Davis said he did not wish to appear as "impeaching the intelligence or integrity of any member of the jury" but believed that some of them "were mystified by the phase of the case relating to the question of arson, and therefore the counsel for the defense has moved for a new trial and a stay of proceedings."

AFTER BARBER WAS CALLED into court on October 30, Davis moved for a new trial on the grounds that the verdict was contrary to the evidence, the jury's conduct was illegal in rendering two verdicts, a juror had conducted himself improperly in leaving the jury box without the court's permission during the trial and the court erred in its decisions on the admissibility of evidence and in the charge to the jury on questions of law and fact. The court denied the motion and sentenced Barber to be hanged on December 18. Without a quiver of a muscle or change of countenance, Barber quietly followed the sheriff to the jail. "For all evidence of feeling shown during the entire trial," commented the *Journal*, "he might have been the casual witness of a *drama* instead of the chief actor in the *tragedy*."

DAVIS FILED AN APPEAL on December 7. A week before the anniversary of the crime, he told a reporter that Barber was growing worse and had "strange hallucinations" at times, frequently imagining himself "vicegerent of the Saviour, and then again his malady assumes other forms. At intervals he is calm and gentle, but his trouble shows continual progress and exhibits the usual characteristics of epileptic insanity."

The *Journal* of March 9 could not omit a grace note of skepticism: "[Barber's] physical appearance has notably improved since his arrest a year ago. His form is fuller and rounder. His sunken cheeks have filled out, and to ordinary everyday individuals who have seen him he seems to be a very healthy specimen for one afflicted with a life-sapping mental infirmity. To the expert insanity specialist the prisoner may seem a total mental wreck, but to others he seems in the full possession of the average man's physical and mental strength."

Richard Mason died on February 3, 1889, and was buried with Ann at Grove Cemetery, Trumansburg.[106]

Gravestone of Ann and Richard Mason, Grove Cemetery, Trumansburg. *Photo by R. Marcin.*

ON OCTOBER 8, 1889, the court of appeals granted a new trial, but the grounds for this were not stated. When Barber was told the result of his attorney's appeal, "he gave no outward sign of pleasure or satisfaction, but merely nodded his head mechanically."[107] A reporter asked him how he was feeling these days.

"I have not slept well lately."

"Perhaps the news you have just heard will enable you to sleep better."

"I don't know that it will make any difference."

ALTHOUGH THE SENTIMENT PREVAILED that a second trial was necessary, the question of its occurrence was still unresolved in December. By February 12, 1890, the *Ithaca Journal* had determined that "the almost forgotten" Barber "bids fair to die of old age before his case is definitely settled."

Barber's case was at last disposed of on March 18, 1890, in a trial lasting less than two hours. According to the *Journal*, "It seemed to be understood from the outset that the trial was to be mere matter of form and that the verdict was to be 'guilty of murder in the second degree.'"

District Attorney Jennings read a portion of the evidence taken at the first trial and examined a few witnesses to establish the fact of the murder. Davis read from the printed evidence in the case. With no summation from the attorneys, Judge Smith at once charged the jury, which returned with the anticipated verdict.

Barber was sentenced to hard labor in Auburn prison for the term of his natural life, "unless executive clemency interposes in his behalf before the pale horseman calls upon him."[108] Throughout the proceedings, to which he seemed to listen intently, he maintained his characteristic stoic demeanor and displayed no more emotion when sentence was passed on him than he did at his first trial. The *Journal* was satisfied that Barber had "at last received something of his just desserts."

AN ANNOUNCEMENT ON THE *Auburn Advertiser* bulletin board that John Davis, the embezzling former city treasurer of Rochester, had been sentenced to Auburn prison for five years caused a large crowd to assemble at the 10:45 a.m. train on March 27 in hopes of glimpsing the famous criminal.

"When the train from the west stopped at the station, a slender, demure-looking man, wearing a brown suit and spring overcoat stopped off the car, accompanied by a portly, austere-looking and bewhiskered individual who carried a brand new hand bag and kept a careful watch over his slender companion."

"That's Davis," whispered the crowd, but those who "left the prison gate this morning congratulating themselves upon seeing the great embezzler will be pained to learn that they had scrutinized a life-man instead."

While Barber was waiting in the keeper's hall, "his downcast face and compressed lips told of the inward struggle he was making at composure"[109] "Nothing I can say now will help my case in any way," Barber said, "but how can anyone believe I was in my right mind when I made that assault on my two best friends? I never drank stimulants in my life and the only reason for my awful action was a stroke of epilepsy."

Barber was taken below, shaved, given a haircut, changed his clothes for the state uniform and was assigned to a cell. The boy who took care of the warden's office gazed at Barber's sorrowful figure and said, "That man feels 'bouts I did two years ago, but thank goodness I'se only got six months more."

BARBER EXPRESSED HIS GRATITUDE toward his indefatigable attorney and friend George Davis via a skill he learned in prison: in 1892, he made a chair of mahogany and leather, "in every respect a fine piece of work,"[110] for Davis as Christmas gift.

Davis continued to take a deep interest in Barber and believed that his condition and conduct since his incarceration bore out the theory advanced by the defense. In August 1895, he wrote to the superintendent of the Utica State Hospital concerning Barber and received a reply stating, "It is gratifying to have one's theory so fully confirmed by the subsequent facts of the patient's history. The incident to which you call my attention is so thoroughly characteristic of the irresistible impulses of the epileptic, of which he retains no recollection, that there can no longer be any possible doubt as to the unfortunate man's condition."[111]

Chapter 8
CAITANO PANICO

Watkins, Schuyler County
1907

Although they had lived in the same town in Italy, Caitano Panico did not make the acquaintance of Carlina Spirito until they immigrated to the United States. Panico arrived in the village of Watkins (now Watkins Glen) in 1903 at the age of twenty-one and went to work at the Glen salt plant at Salt Point. Two years later, Carlina, then twenty or twenty-one, also left Italy for Watkins, boarding with her sister Nicolina and her husband. She found employment at the same establishment as Panico and, through industriousness and frugality, managed to save $200. The two developed a relationship and after a time became engaged.

Some months afterward, Panico began to work only for a few hours a day and spend what he earned on alcohol. Carlina objected and asked him to do better, but Panico "continued his dissolute habits."[112] He urged Carlina to marry him and use her savings to purchase household goods. She told him she would carry out her promise of marriage if he improved his conduct and saved his money. Panico persisted with his shiftless, intemperate ways, and Carlina broke off the engagement.

Another migrant from their town who settled in Watkins was Chauncey Zuccarelle, who had been Carlina's amour in Italy. He had been in the United States since 1901 and was joined three years later by his sixteen-year-old sister Mary, who boarded with another sister of Carlina, Cataline. In

1906, he sued Carlina for forty dollars that he had sent to her while she was still in Italy but lost the suit. This apparently did not spawn enmity between them, for on Easter Sunday, March 31, 1907, Zuccarelle and Carlina spent most of the evening dancing together at a fete. Panico, who was also present, claimed that this did not anger him and believed he would have trouble with Zuccarelle if he intervened. Carlina did not speak to him.

Monday, April 1, Panico came into the sewing room at the salt plant two or three times and sat on a barrel at one end of the table where Carlina was working, silently watching her. Each time he spoke to another employee "in an ordinary and usual tone of voice."[113]

At 5:00 p.m., Carlina was called downstairs to sew bags, and Panico followed her. No one knew what words they exchanged, but their voices were not raised.

Half an hour later, Carlina returned to the sewing room for her wraps, with Panico about fifty feet behind her. Mary Zuccarelle and Carlina's thirteen-year-old niece Lucy were the only other occupants of the room. Panico stopped her as she started to leave. "What are you in such a hurry for? I wish to talk to you."

"It's too late, I must go home."

"Do you remember what I told you in February?" he asked. Carlina replied in the negative.

"I will make you remember!" Panico shouted before he slapped her face. Mary grabbed Panico's coat and tried to hold him until Carlina got away, but he pulled from her grasp, grabbed Carlina by the shoulder, kicked her and flung her onto the conveyor belt. Mary seized a shovel and hit Panico across the back. He jerked the shovel from her hands, sprang at Carlina, drew a knife and slashed at her face and neck. Mary struck Panico on the head with a broom, but at the sight of blood flying everywhere, she fled outside and gave the alarm. Lucy ran crying from the room, and Panico followed her, escaping by the north door while Lucy headed in the opposite direction.

Carlina staggered into the pan room, blood coating her face. Two men caught her as she was about to fall and let her down easily.

Joseph Harvey saw Panico rush out the door and look back as he crossed the footbridge and again when he reached the railroad tracks. Shortly thereafter, another man came downstairs and said that one of the girls was badly cut and lying on the floor of the pan room.

A trail of blood led from the sewing room to where Carlina lay on the floor; two women were wiping blood from her face. Blood had spattered a stool, table, sacks and other articles and saturated Carlina's dress.

Harvey walked across the tracks to phone Dr. J.F. Barnes, who was soon at the scene. He found Carlina in an improvised bed, nearly unconscious and bleeding profusely from her severed right carotid artery. A long gash had lain open her left cheek, exposing the bone. She had two long cuts on her right cheek and several smaller ones, most of which were to the bone. About a quart of coagulated blood covered the floor where she'd fallen.

Barnes had her taken to a house across the tracks and placed in a warm room. He ligated the artery, sewed up the wounds, gave her heart tonics and stayed with her for three hours before leaving her in the care of several women. Carlina died quietly around 1:30 a.m.

Sheriff Thompson, who had been notified of the assault at once, sent word to all surrounding towns and villages with a description of Panico: short, thick-set, curly black hair parted in the middle, dark mustache and dressed in a dark suit, white shirt, soft hat and blue handkerchief around his neck instead of a collar. On April 2, word was received that a man answering his description had been seen at Beaver Dams. Deputy Sheriff Karl Loomis and Constable David Field drove there at once, where they found Panico on a bench at the depot, guarded by several people, at 2:00 a.m. on April 3. He did not resist arrest.

Salt plant on Seneca Lake, Watkins Glen. *Library of Congress.*

On the way to the jail in Watkins, Panico told Field, "My brother want me marry girl in old country. Me no like her, me like Lena." If he liked Lena, why did he cut her, Field asked. "Lena make me mad. She marry me, then she no marry me."

When the prisoner was searched at the jail, a rusty jackknife was found on his person. When asked if the knife were the one with which he'd cut Carlina, Panico said, "That's all me have."

CARLINA'S FUNERAL WAS HELD on April 3 at St. Mary's of the Lake Catholic Church, only a few rods from the jail. Panico heard the bell but did not know for whom it was tolling, as he was unaware that Carlina was dead. The services were "attended by a large concourse of sympathizing friends," and her casket "was literally buried with flowers, attesting to her popularity."[114]

Much rancorous feeling against Panico was exhibited, especially by the Italians employed at the saltworks, who "gather[ed] in the streets in large numbers and excitedly discuss[ed] the tragedy."[115] Sheriff Thompson, fearing trouble, refused admittance to the crowds congregating at the jail.

AFTER A PRIVATE INQUEST in the grand jury room on Thursday, April 4, Coroner Post decided that Carlina Spirito came to her death by criminal means at the hands of Caitano Panico. The defendant was brought into the room and formally charged with murder in the first degree. When the interpreter stated the charge to him, "he shuddered visibly but did not utter

Gravestone of Carollinna (Carlina) Spirito, St. Mary's Cemetery, Watkins Glen. *Photo by R. Marcin.*

a word."[116] Counsel for the prisoner, former judge O.P. Hurd, entered a plea of not guilty, and the examination was set for Monday.

The officials, fearing a demonstration from the scores of Italians waiting outside, brought the prisoner across the jail enclosures and had him enter the grand jury room through a window. He was taken back to his cell the same way.

At Monday's hearing, the same witnesses were sworn and repeated their stories. Post held Panico for the action of the grand jury on the charge of first-degree murder, which carried a penalty of death.

In subsequent weeks, crowds demanding to see Panico continued to descend on the jail, much to Sheriff Thompson's vexation. "The most annoying of them are the women who seem to be persistent in their request," the *Watkins Review* reported on April 17. "One woman explained the other day she wanted to kiss the prisoner."

As for Panico, since his confinement he had been "the most orderly prisoner in the bunch," according to the *Elmira Star-Gazette*. "He refuses to discuss the murder and has little to say in regard to anything."[117]

SCHUYLER COUNTY'S FIRST MURDER trial since 1863 opened on Tuesday, December 17, with Justice Albert Gladding presiding. When court convened, the room was crowded to its doors, and even standing room was scarce.

Thompson brought Panico into court at 2:15 p.m. and conducted him to his seat. The prisoner appeared "nervous and pale and never for a moment allowed his eyes to wander toward any of his Italian friends."[118] Fifty-six jurors were examined, several of whom were dismissed for their objection to capital punishment.

District Attorney Velie, assisted by attorney B.W. Nye, opened the case for the people on Wednesday, in what the *Watkins Review* called "a model of conciseness and brevity," speaking for fifteen minutes. He outlined the "tragic story" and "regarded it as a fact highly complimentary to American citizenship, that of the jurors examined each one testified that, if accepted, he would give the alien defendant as fair a trial as if he were an American citizen, unswerved by any prejudice as to his nativity."[119] The crime, he stated, was a clear and unmistakable case of premeditated murder, as Panico's conduct and words indicated.

Mary Zuccarelle, called to the stand, said she had told Panico fifteen or sixteen days before the murder that Carlina did not like him and would not marry him. Cross-examined by Hurd, she denied that she had been trying to get Carlina to leave Panico and marry her brother. Hurd asked her about a song she was singing the afternoon of April 1 containing something about "first love being best love" and another song with the words "The first love is like a stain, the more you wash the longer it stays. The second love is like a bride, the more you wash, the more it goes away." She replied that it was an Italian song often sung in the home country. It included the name Caitano but had no reference to the defendant. Hurd attempted to show that Mary had been singing the song to taunt Panico, but she denied it, claiming that she did not know he was in the room when she began the song. She said she habitually sang while at work.

According to Dr. Barnes, Carlina's death resulted from shock and loss of blood. On cross-examination, he said the heart tonics he'd given consisted of digitalis, belladonna and strychnine, all poisonous if taken in sufficient quantities. Hurd insinuated that the medicines, rather than Panico's knife, might have been responsible for Carlina's death. Barnes that said the remedies were "proper," and he believed the nurse he left in charge was competent.

Matteo Martine spoke without an interpreter, but his testimony was obtained with difficulty as his English was far from fluent. Panico boarded at his house about twenty days before Carlina was killed. Martine asked Panico on several occasions why he didn't go to work and received the reply, "I don't feel good." Martine once told him, "If you want to marry Carlina you must go to work and get money." Panico said Carlina had money and could buy many things.

Cataline said that Carlina came to her house once when Panico boarded there. Panico became angry and told her, "Catalina, you step between us every time. To --- with you!"

Nicolina's husband said that Panico came to his house on Saturday, March 30, but Carlina left him and went upstairs. He claimed that Panico had tried to borrow money from him to marry Carlina.

Nicolina said she overheard Carlina tell Panico last Palm Sunday that she would marry him if he would work and save money. She denied that she'd tried to make trouble between them.

Chauncey Zuccarelle had told Panico on March 30, "Go to work, make money and Carlina will marry you." Panico had replied, "You're fooling me; you'll marry her yourself." Zuccarelle said no. He had never spoken to Carlina of marriage, nor did he come here expecting to marry her, as they "were only in love."

Angelo Copolell, an employee at the Glen Salt Works, had worked with Panico in March. When he told Panico that Carlina sent her regards to him, Panico said, "I'll give my regards to her and make her remember."

Field repeated the conversation he'd had with Panico on the way to Watkins, saying that Panico had asked twice if Carlina were dead. Hurd claimed that Panico did not speak English at all, and therefore this exchange could not have taken place. Field asserted that Panico spoke broken English and could be understood by those familiar with him. The people's case rested.

In his opening statement, Hurd said that Panico had committed a crime and deserved to be punished, but he was not guilty of murder in the first degree and the penalty should not be death. The people had proven nothing more than manslaughter, nor did they establish premeditation and design. Hurd "commented upon the fiery temperament characteristic of the Latin peoples, and alluded briefly to the mad love, the almost insane infatuation of Panico for the girl he murdered; jealous passion bred of an instant a murderous hatred, and at that instant the deed was done. Responsible? No. Insane? Yes, declared the attorney with ringing eloquence."[120]

Cainano Viechione and Panico's older half brother, Raphele Volpe, testified to Panico's good conduct and reputation; under cross-examination, they admitted he drank some.

The defendant, "nervous but determined," took the stand. "Well knowing that his life hangs in the balance, he made his answers guardedly, briefly, never taking his eyes from attorney and interpreter for an instant."[121]

Panico said that he was twenty-five years old and could not read or

write. He had met Carlina while he was living at Mr. Spirito's house and walked to and from work with her when he'd had the time. He detailed his courtship of her and their engagement. She had him send to Italy for proof that his parents, both of whom were dead, were married, and when shown the certificate, she'd shrugged and said, "The papers have come, now you must look for money." He said they were still going together at that time.

He had gone to the saltworks around 1:00 p.m. or 2:00 p.m. on April 1. Carlina would not talk to him but "was singing a song against" him. He returned about 4:00 p.m. or 5:00 p.m. and spoke to her. She said, "Don't talk to me; I don't want to see you any more." This was at 5:10 p.m. He saw her again at 5:20 p.m. and said, "What are you in such a hurry for? I wish to talk with you." Panico continued:

Caitano Panico. *From the* Elmira Star Gazette, *December 20, 1907.*

I then said: "You know how old I am and know how old you are and there is no use of making so many lies. I won't make any more trouble. My brother want to send girl from old country. If you had told me first, I would have never bothered you."

I said, "You trusted me like a pirate, and you ask me to follow you all the time, but you was in love with the first love."

She said, "You had better not think of me any more."

I replied, "I WILL MARK YOU SO NOBODY WILL MARRY YOU; YOU WILL HAVE TO MARRY ME."

Then I got mad, made the marks on her and got away.

"I did not intend to kill her," he insisted. "Mary Zuccarelle struck me with a shovel, I don't know where. I was greatly excited—confusion in my head....I had no idea I killed her. I intended to come back to Watkins. I did not know Carlina was dead until the sheriff told it."

The *Watkins Review* characterized Nye's cross-examination as "most searching and exhaustive." Nye had made Panico rehearse the story he'd told the day before, but this time he gave it with variations.

Panico said he did not remember kicking or slapping Carlina and intended to make one mark on her. Nye asked, "Then why did you strike her at least 10 times?"

"I don't know how I came to be blind."

When asked why he ran away if he only "marked" Carlina, Panico said he was afraid his countrymen would "lick" him. Earlier, when Hurd asked him if he was afraid of being attacked by Italians, he had said he was not.

Before the defense closed at 11:30 a.m. on Friday, Panico was shown some pictures of the dead woman. "He took them and scrutinized them closely without flinching."[122]

In his summation for the prisoner, Hurd centered his argument on the case for manslaughter. He emphasized Panico's prior good reputation and said that it should bear on the jury's verdict.

Nye, according to the *Watkins Review*, made "a splendid plea for the people." Panico, he claimed, had not only intended to kill Carlina—he had also premeditated the act. He became angry and jealous when Carlina deemed him unfit to be her life companion and dogged her footsteps until the opportunity came to strike the fatal blow. If he meant only to mar or disfigure her, why did he cut her "again and again, until 10 horrible wounds had been made and the blood was flying in all directions?" Could any man on the jury believe a man would butcher a girl like that if he did not mean to kill her?

Nye pointed out that premeditation was not necessarily a case of weeks, days or hours, but may be for a few moments—long enough to choose between doing or not doing the deed. "If ever there was a case of cruel, willful, deliberate and atrocious murder, this is one."

Gladding's charge to the jury was brief. He did not review the testimony, but rather defined degrees of murder and manslaughter and explained "reasonable doubt." The jury retired at 4:30 p.m.

On the first few ballots, the jury was divided between murder in the first degree, murder in the second degree and one or two for manslaughter. When the jury members returned to court at 9:20 a.m. on Saturday, they asked that the two degrees of murder be explained again. At 11:00 a.m., they returned a verdict of guilty of murder in the second degree.

Panico received an indeterminate sentence, with a minimum of twenty years at Auburn State Prison—the maximum was the term of his natural life. He did not appear affected by either the verdict or the sentence. On December 23, Thompson escorted Panico to Auburn State Prison. Under a new law, he could obtain his freedom in twenty years by good behavior.

IN A BIZARRE POSTSCRIPT to the case, Carlina's sister Mary Spirito was boarding with her brother-in-law in February 1908 when shots were fired at her through the window. Mary escaped injury and had a warrant issued for the arrest of Millio Dilalle, who, she said, persisted in "making love to her against her will" and offered her $300 if she would become his wife.[123]

Chapter 9
JAMES WILLIAMS

Lima, Livingston County
1911

Before his household became the locus of what a Geneseo newspaper called "one of the darkest and foulest crimes ever committed in this state," James Duffy had been known as the first from the town of Pittsford to enlist in the Union army. In 1911, the seventy-two-year-old farmer was living in a small settlement locally known as "Smithtown," between Honeoye Falls and North Bloomfield, with Elizabeth Webb, his sister-in-law and housekeeper, and his seventeen-year-old granddaughter, Verna Duffy, whom he had raised since her infancy, after the death of her mother.

At about 7:15 p.m. on Saturday, February 18, Duffy was playing cards with Verna when someone knocked on the door. Webb remarked that it was probably the boy with the evening paper, and Duffy told the person to enter.

Into the house stepped a stranger, a young African American man with a club in one hand and a revolver in the other. He approached Duffy and asked, "Have you got any money?"

Duffy, fearing no harm, rose from his seat. "Why, yes, lots of it," he replied laughingly. "How much do you want?" He had hardly spoken the words when the stranger put the revolver in his pocket, whirled his club aloft with both hands and brought it down on Duffy's head, knocking him to the floor and breaking the weapon in two.

Webb told Verna to run after help and started for the side door as Verna dashed toward the front entrance. The moment Webb reached the side porch, the intruder struck her over the head.

Verna had fled halfway across the street when the man caught her by the arm and dealt her a blow that cut her scalp. As she struggled to escape, he choked off her frantic screams for help. She broke free and ran back to the porch, but he caught her again and half-carried, half-dragged her to the back of the barn behind the house, throwing her to the ground and choking her whenever she tried to scream. He ripped at her clothes, tearing some off entirely, including her undergarments. Her assailant asked if she knew him, and she replied, "No." She then managed to scream with enough force to frighten him away.

Although her arm had been broken and she was severely bruised, Verna made her way to the house, where her grandfather lay covered with blood. She took him to the kitchen, bathed his head with water and washed the blood from his face. He was alive but unconscious. Webb was in the dining room, badly stunned from the blow. The knot of hair on top of her head had absorbed the brunt and likely saved her life. When she became conscious, she found herself seated in a chair surrounded by neighbors.

A doctor was summoned "and made all as comfortable as possible."[124] Also at the scene that night were Deputy Sheriff George Root and two constables. Verna seemed dazed and could not give coherent answers to their questions, but the blood throughout the house provided clear evidence of the crime. A set of tracks reached the window, as if someone had been looking in at the occupants. An imprint of one of the shoes showed five large nails in the heel, and these led to the home of Jesse Hall, an African American man of Honeoye Falls.

When Deputy Sheriff Wilton called at Hall's that evening, one of his tenants, James Williams, told Hall if they asked for him to say he wasn't there—he'd had trouble with Quintus Lewis, and perhaps the officers were in search of him. (According to the *Livingston Republican* of June 8, "Quintus Lewis is a harmless and peaceable colored man living in Honeoye Falls, and never would engage in trouble of any sort with anyone.") Williams was arrested and taken to Verna Duffy for identification, but she could not say positively that he was the one.

THE NEXT DAY, ROOT returned to Honeoye Falls, called on a friend of Verna's and plied her with questions. He learned that "a negro" who was cleaning the church furnace had smiled at the two girls when they passed him. The girl added that she had seen the same man, with a club in his hand, going toward the Duffy home that evening. After further investigation, Root learned that the man who cleaned the furnace was James Williams.

Root informed Wilton of his discovery, but Wilton assured him that he had Williams before Verna Duffy the night before and she failed to identify him. This did not satisfy Root, who believed that another visit to Williams was in order.

As Root, Wilton and Constable Walter McLaughlin approached Hall's residence, they saw a man through the window whom McLaughlin identified as Williams. Hall admitted them when they knocked, but Williams had left the room.

Root was conducted to Williams's quarters, where he found the suspect. He told Williams to stay with the two other men for a few moments while he searched the apartment. Under the bed, he discovered a coat, overalls and a pair of shoes, all covered with blood. Williams, upon being asked whose they were and how blood got on them, said they were Hall's and the blood came from meat he'd been carrying. Hall called Williams a liar and said that he had never worn the coat in his life. He had found it in a barrel of old papers he had drawn away from a store in Honeoye Falls, he said, and had given it to Williams a few days before, so he would not spoil his good clothes while cleaning a cistern. He further told Root that Williams had worn the coat and overalls all day Saturday.

This was enough for Root, who arrested Williams and took him to the Duffy residence. Williams, afraid of being mobbed, asked him not to go in. This time, both Elizabeth Webb and Verna Duffy recognized him as the intruder.

Root delivered Williams to Sheriff Wilcox, who brought him to the county jail at Geneseo. While waiting for the train, Williams confessed but claimed that he was "loaded with cocaine" at the time of the incident. The *Avon News* proclaimed, "The man who sold or gave Williams the cocaine should be compelled to suffer some penalty, as undoubtedly he is indirectly guilty of the crime."[125]

JAMES DUFFY DIED ON February 21, never regaining consciousness. An autopsy revealed that his skull had been fractured to the roof of the mouth immediately behind the nose. The examiners concluded that death was due to inflammation and congestion of the brain.

Gravestone of James Duffy, West Bloomfield Rural Cemetery. *Photo by R. Marcin.*

Since his arrest, reported the *Syracuse Journal*, Williams had "become almost a raving maniac. Whether the man's mind is really unbalanced, or whether his condition results from fear, long debauch and enforced abstinence from cocaine, remains to be determined."[126]

Quintus Lewis, whom Williams implicated in his confession before he began raving, was also taken into custody. Lewis denied having any knowledge of the assault, although he admitted to having been with Williams Saturday afternoon. "I'm a lucky child that I'm not being arrested down South for anything like this," Lewis remarked. He was soon released.

ON FEBRUARY 23, THE day of Duffy's funeral, the *Syracuse Journal* noted that "the strapping, big colored man" had ceased his ravings "and evidently thinks his case is hopeless, as he has asked for a minister."

Williams had not been informed of the condition of his victim, and the attendant thought to keep him quiet by assuring him that Duffy was not only alive, but improving. Williams insisted, however, "That old man died over there"—he could "feel it in his bones."

"Williams is still suffering from what appears to be fright, and evidently from the effects of debauch," stated the *Journal.* "He jumps at every sound that reaches him from the outside, and seems to fear that a mob may undertake to remove him from the jail."

With newspapers employing every known synonym to convey the "savagery" and "depravity" of the crime, the *Journal* underscored the subhuman status of its alleged perpetrator, complete with the sixth sense attributed to such entities. He was nonetheless sentient enough to realize the consequences of his actions, lest anyone conclude that such a state rendered him irresponsible:

> *Williams is described as looking more like a savage beast than a human being and the sheriff is wondering if there is such a thing as mental transmission, with mental telegraph wires running from the jail to the murdered man's home.... When he does speak his voice sounds like a growl. The fear that he continually manifests is regarded as evidence that he realizes his predicament and what the punishment for his crime will probably be.*[127]

On Wednesday, May 31, a special term of Supreme Court convened in Geneseo, with Justice George Benton presiding, at which Williams was placed on trial for what the *Livingston Democrat* called "one of the most brutal and fiendish crimes ever committed in this county."[128] The prosecution was conducted by District Attorney Frank Cook, assisted by Fred Quirk. Williams was defended by Charles Newton, "one of the most successful criminal lawyers in this part of the state," assisted by William Flynn, "who has interested himself in the colored man from the start."[129] Williams's attorneys admitted that he had done the deed, and "it was simply a question as to whether he was of so low a degree of intelligence that he was responsible for what he had done and should be treated as an insane man rather than a desperate murderer."[130]

There could hardly be any suspense about Williams's fate. The confident *Livingston Democrat* announced that "a network of convincing evidence has been woven about the criminal from which it seemed that it was impossible for him to escape. Nothing was left undone in order to fasten the responsibility for the crime upon Williams, and the evidence was of the most conclusive nature."[131] With its reference to the defendant as "the brute" and assertion that his original intent upon entering the house was undoubtedly the assault of Verna Duffy, on whom he'd pounced "like a dog upon a rat," there was no question of the outcome for which the *Democrat* hoped.

Predictably, the courtroom was filled with spectators, "many of whom were anxious to hear the details of the revolting crime, and there seemed to be a diversity of opinion as to whether or not Williams was insane when the crime was committed, the majority being of the opinion that he was mentally responsible for his acts on the night in question."[132]

Webb, though more than eighty years of age, "told a clear and intelligent story and could not be shaken by a racking cross examination."[133] She had a scant memory of what occurred after she had been struck on the head but identified Williams as the man who came into the house.

Hall said he had known Williams for the past two years and told of the circumstances under which Williams came to live with him. On the day of the murder, Williams had been shoveling snow from the streets. He came to Hall's home, borrowed a quarter, left and did not come back until about 6:00 p.m., at which time he came in and got some matches. When Mrs. Hall asked him to take supper, he replied that he did not care for any and left the house.

Williams returned around 8:00 p.m., sat by the stove for a short time, got up, washed his hands and went to bed. It was between the hours of 6:00 p.m. and 8:00 p.m. that the crime was committed.

Before long, Hall heard a knock at the door and, upon opening it, found Constable Daniel Russell. Russell did not tell Hall what happened but said he would be back shortly. Mrs. Hall inquired what Russell wanted, and when his name was mentioned, Williams spoke from his room, saying, "If he asks for me tell him I am not here."

Russell returned and asked for Williams, telling Hall that Duffy had been murdered and they thought Williams had done it. Williams got up and wanted to put on Hall's shoes, saying they were his, but Mrs. Hall said, "No you don't; put on your own." Williams went out, came back after a while and said that he did not see why they should think he did it. He went to bed, but several men

Frank Cook, Fred Quirk, Charles Newton and William Flynn. *From the Livingston Democrat, June 7, 1911.*

came back to take Williams to Duffy's to see if Verna could identify him. He returned a little later, announcing that the girl said he was not the one. Hall heard nothing more about the matter until the next day, when officers came to arrest Williams.

Quintus Lewis was accused of furnishing the defendant with cocaine, which he vigorously denied.

After Verna Duffy took the stand, the prosecution rested its case on Thursday afternoon. During the trial, the *Democrat* noted, "the defendant appeared to be composed, although at times he appeared to be somewhat nervous, but that was natural, as any person being tried for a crime of that character would have nerves of iron if he betrayed no mental feeling."

In opening his case, Newton said that the defendant had fits at various times throughout his life during which he had been devoid of understanding and knew nothing of his actions. He said he would leave it to the jurors to decide whether their verdict would be one that meant a death sentence, or one whereby the defendant would be confined and cared for in view of his unsound mind.

Williams was sworn and "told the story of his life in a rambling, unintelligent way."[134] He had been born in Maryland twenty-one years before and did not remember ever seeing his father; his mother died when he was very young. At an early age, he left the town in which he was born and went to Baltimore, where he lived for a number of years at the home of a white woman, Mrs. Scott, and did odd jobs about her place. Mrs. Scott and her two daughters moved to Richmond and took him with them; he did not know how old he was at the time. From there, he went with them to New York City, where he worked at a stable for about seven months.

To show the jury that the defendant was "pretty near a natural-born fool and couldn't be relied upon to distinguish as between right and wrong,"[135] his attorney handed him a fifty-cent piece and asked him what it was. Williams said, "A dollar." He then identified a dollar bill as a two-dollar bill. Asked if he could read, he said, "I can read a little printing." When requested to recite the alphabet, he got as far as *E* several times and could not go any further. He counted up to nine before being unable to continue. According to the *Journal*, "The impression generally formed was that the negro was acting a part."

Williams then told about going from one city to another in New Jersey and New York and working for a short period on adjoining farms. When about fourteen years old, he became ill and sought admittance to a hospital, where it was discovered he had lung trouble. He later went back to New

York and was arrested for stealing a horse in New Jersey. He was sent to a reform school at Trenton and there received his first education, at the age of about sixteen.

After being released from reform school, he worked on a sailboat and then at a hotel in Rochester. Not liking it there, he went to a labor bureau, paid one dollar and obtained employment at a farm in Mumford. After a while, he went back to the labor bureau, from where he was sent to Honeoye Falls.

At this time, Williams said, a girl at the house where he was working asked him to run away with her and marry her. He took a horse from the barn, and they went to the next town to get married. He told a boy to bring the horse back, but before the marriage could take place, Williams was arrested and "sent up" for stealing the horse. He was released last November and treated at a hospital for pneumonia. After he recovered, the hospital officials bought him a ticket for Honeoye Falls, and he was sent there sometime in the winter. Williams said that he was subject to dizzy spells, "when he did not know what was going on."[136]

Questioned in regard to Duffy's murder, Williams seemed "undisturbed, and spoke in the same manner as he had through the examination."[137] He had a vague recollection of being in a fight at Honeoye Falls but had no memory of whom he fought or on what occasion.

The next witnesses, two men of Honeoye Falls for whom Williams had worked, said when they paid him he recognized the value of money and was able to distinguish the different pieces.

James Williams. *From the Nunda News, June 10, 1911.*

Dr. A.P. Reed testified that Williams had fits in his cell, which, though not necessarily epileptic, showed many of the same symptoms. The prisoner did not foam at the mouth, but rather bit the bars of his cell and tried to tear them loose. When Williams was in these conditions, he thought a mob was pursuing him. Attorney Flynn said that he had seen Williams in eight or nine fits during his visits to the jail. William Crowley, superintendent of a home under the auspices of the Volunteers of America, stated that Williams had registered there and that he recognized his signature. The prosecution thus scored a point, as Williams had testified that he could not write.

Dr. Edwin Hanes, an insanity expert, described the four forms of epilepsy: grand mal, petit mal, Jacksonian and physical. In the first three forms, Williams could not possibly have committed the act charged against him, as he would have no control over his muscles; in the fourth, it was possible for a patient to be apparently entirely rational and yet be in a state of epilepsy for as long as a year and then, upon recovering from the seizure, have no recollection of anything he did during that time. In this condition, impulsiveness predominates one's actions, and one may commit violent acts.

Dr. Reed, recalled by the district attorney, was of the opinion that it was impossible for Williams to have committed the crimes while in a state similar to the seizures he'd had at the jail.

Drs. Frederick Sefton and Wallace Harriman, two specialists in nervous disorders, agreed that Williams's attacks might have been caused by fright-induced hysteria and even in that event the seizures could have continued until May, "a point which the defense seemed to doubt."[138] Here the defense rested.

Summations began on Saturday morning. Newton made "a strong plea for Williams, admitting his commission of the act, but urging that he was entirely irresponsible and was in a state of physical epilepsy, with no knowledge of what he was doing. His remarks occupied about 50 minutes and he certainly did all that lawyer ever did for client in using every weapon in the arsenal of eloquence and argument to obtain a verdict in his behalf."[139]

Cook had less to say in his reply, consuming only twenty-five minutes, "but he tore every defense that had been set up to shreds, showing that low cunning on the part of the Negro had been the guiding spirit in all his acts, he showed how the man's failure to count, to write and do other simple things was merely a sham, as signatures had been produced written in a clear hand before the tests on the trial, and the defendant had counted to 20 without any mistake for Dr. Reed." Cook "laughed in scorn at the term 'physical epilepsy' referring to it with contemptuous sarcasm and quoting it in derisive tones at the close of several statements offered by him as arguments to show the low cunning and crafty schemes of Williams."[140]

Judge Benton's charge to the jury was, according to the *Democrat*, one of the most impartial ever given in Livingston County, "but we believe at the close of the testimony even, the jurors had their mind made up as to their duty in the matter."[141] They were out only an hour before they returned. The spectators, perhaps anticipating a short wait, had remained in their seats.

Williams appeared slightly agitated as he was brought in, rubbing his hands together but showing no other signs of anxiety. The foreman said that they had found the defendant guilty of murder in the first degree, committed while in the act of attempting to commit a felony, the crime of rape. Williams seemed to take the verdict coolly and stood in the prisoner's box with a dispassionate expression.

Williams stated that he had no cause to show why the sentence should not be pronounced. Benton said the penalty was fixed by statute and that it remained for the court merely to set the time in carrying it out. Williams was to remain in Auburn prison until, on a day set by the warden the week of July 17, he would be electrocuted.

Williams asked if he might speak, and Benton granted him the privilege. In a shaky, gasping voice, the defendant said he had no remembrance of having killed Duffy, but Benton told him that the jury had heard that story and did not believe it.

Before anyone could restrain him, Williams pulled a razor from his pocket and slashed his throat from ear to ear. As blood gushed forth, spectators screamed and fled the room.

Deputy Root threw himself on Williams, caught his arm and shouted, "Take that out of his hand! Get it away from him!" "Tremendous excitement almost bordering on panic reigned," noted the *Republican*, but "officers made no attempt to restore order as they were too busy grappling with the defendant." After a brief struggle, the sheriff, deputies and several spectators managed to get the razor away from Williams, who was handcuffed and taken to jail. An examination of the wound revealed that it was not a serious one, although it pained him considerably. Williams told the men gathered about him that he preferred death at his own hands to the electric chair.

Both the *Democrat* and *Republican* believed that Williams's shrewdness in concealing the razor must have been extraordinary; Sheriff Wilcox had been informed several weeks before that he had a razor, but thorough searches of his cell failed to reveal the hiding place, and Wilcox was convinced that Williams had nothing of the sort. The *Republican* added, "If he intended to kill himself he chose a most inopportune place to do it, as he made the attempt in a crowded court room where there was every chance of his being prevented."

After the wound was treated, Wilcox and Root escorted Williams to Auburn. According to the *Democrat*, "He gave the officers more or less trouble on the way down. He managed to bite one of the deputies."

The *Auburn Citizen* claimed that Williams weakened as he neared the prison walls, "and for the first time seemed to feel his position."[142] A crowd had gathered at the depot Saturday night in hopes of catching a glimpse of the condemned man; at the sight, Williams cowered against his guards. He regained his nerve after the short walk to the gate and ascended the steps with more confidence. His wound was dressed, and he was given a cell in the condemned row.

THE GENESEO PAPERS COULD not have been more satisfied with the efforts of the prosecution, on whom they heaped paragraphs of gratitude and praise. "When Williams goes to the electric chair one of the worst criminals that ever invaded Livingston county will pay the penalty of his crime," the *Democrat* exulted. "[T]he people of this county have the satisfaction of knowing that crimes of that character will not go unpunished and law and justice will prevail regardless of those who may have opposite views."

Newton "did all in his power for his client, but we believe that he was convinced from the start that he was working in a hopeless cause."

The *Republican* referred to the trial as "a solemn and an awful thing," but it was everything the defendant could have asked for in the way of fairness and justness. "Had the crime been committed in the South, Williams would have paid the penalty so often paid by members of his race and been burned at the stake or hanged to the nearest tree; and even in this state and county, civilized and enlightened as we claim to be, there was strong talk of just such a procedure at the time and place of his crime. But happily such a disgrace was saved by cooler counsel."

The fact that premeditated murder had not been established was of no consequence, the *Republican* assured its readers, for rumors and emotions trumped facts and the law:

> *Some of the details of his crime are so repulsive and revolting that they have no place in the public prints, and in fact they were not brought out on the trial, and others of them were touched upon only very lightly. The jury did not know of them; they are the things that are told only by one man to another and in whispers but never by a witness in open court nor even by a man to his wife. Had the jury known the full story the verdict would probably have been reached in about three minutes, for in spite of oaths and obligations, in spite of solemn charges not to be influenced by passion or prejudice, a juryman could not be a human being and put such matters from his mind in order to deal fairly with a defendant. The district attorney spoke with an intensity which he could poorly conceal when he opened up his summing up remarks by saying that he was there to plead for the American home and its sanctity.*[143]

After his conviction, Williams told Flynn, "I do not remember having killed him. I believe I have had a fair trial, and, if they want to kill me, then all right. I have made peace with my Lord, and am ready to suffer if it is His will. I hate to leave Sheriff Wilcox though; he has been good to me."

IN THE ABSENCE OF evidence that the murder was premeditated, Benton had charged the jury that the assault on Verna Duffy, which was a separate crime, could be taken into account. It was on these grounds that Newton and Flynn planned to file an appeal. This was expected to give Williams a stay of execution until autumn at least, but it took the court a year to get to the case. In late June 1912, it affirmed the conviction and death sentence, which was to be carried out the week of August 12.

Williams attempted suicide once more while in prison, and his condition was such that Warden Benham, who believed Williams insane, reported his actions to the superintendent of prisons. The superintendent referred the matter to Governor Dix, who granted a respite until the week of September 16 and appointed a commission to examine the prisoner's sanity. When informed of Dix's decision, Williams "showed little emotion and sat in his cell in the same lifeless manner that has characterized his appearance for months."[144] According to the *Auburn Citizen*, the opinion prevailed that Williams was insane, in which case he would be transferred to the asylum at Matteawan.

The examination was conducted on August 13 and the report sent to the governor. On September 12, it was announced that the commission had determined that Williams was not insane. In light of the commissioners' comments when they were at the prison, this came as a surprise to local officials. While Williams belonged in the mentally defective class, the report stated, he was sane within the meaning of the statute and should be electrocuted. Dix declined to interfere, and that evening a prison employee told Williams that he would die the next week. Williams nodded to show he understood and then "assumed an expression of stolid indifference and stared vacantly."[145]

ON MONDAY, SEPTEMBER 16, the day before the execution, Williams spent a restless day in his cell. He obtained some comfort in the evening from a talk with Reverend John Hickey, although at times he scarcely seemed to comprehend the clergyman's words. Williams retired shortly after 8:00 p.m.

The *Auburn Semi-Weekly Journal* of September 17 painted this evocative portrait of the *mise en scène* for the execution:

> *The morning, like most other mornings upon which executions are held, was a dark and gloomy one. A gray and ominous sky overhung the city and an oppressive and tomb-like silence prevailed about the grim battlements of the prison. Few people were abroad and as the hour of the execution approached the tread of the column of witnesses making their way into the prison, sounded loud and hollow in the early morning stillness.*

At 5:55 a.m., Benham appeared in the back hall of the administration building and instructed the witnesses to form a column. They filed out into the back yard and through the dynamo room, to the death chamber, where they were quickly seated.

When the guards opened the door of Williams's cell, the two visiting clergymen stepped into the hall. Williams held back. The priests led him gently but firmly from the cell, but he resisted and begged the attendants not to take him to the chair.

Still hesitating, Williams took up the march, a priest on either side. The muscles of his partially folded arms were drawn tense, and he clenched his fists so that his nails pierced the skin. As he walked, his legs shook, and he spoke incoherently, muttering prayers and pleading not to be killed. A guard snatched a soft cap off his head as the group entered the death chamber.

Williams glanced at the chair that awaited him but had no time for a careful examination. He seemed too frightened to sit down, so the guards grasped his shoulder and gently forced him into position.

He scanned the faces of the twenty-two witnesses and attempted to stand, but the straps restrained him. "Don't kill me," he pleaded, his voice trembling and words strangling in his throat. "Gentlemen, don't kill me." His words flowed rapidly and as if he were in a delirium. "I want to warn you all, keep away from the wimmins, keep away from the girls, gentlemen. That's what got me here. That's my voice. Lord Jesus. I am the one." He paused as if expecting his speech to be acknowledged and then almost shouted, "Hello! I'm the one, gentlemen, but don't kill me. Don't kill me. I'm going. Don't kill me, gentlemen."

He was still talking while electrician Edward Davis adjusted the leather mask over his face and wanted to push it away. He pursed his lips and pleaded, "Just a minute."

"That's all right, that's all right," said Davis as he fastened the mask. The guards had bared Williams's left leg to the knee and strapped down his arm. The next instant, there came what the *Semi-Weekly Journal* called "the ominous almost inaudible whine of the death-dealing fluid" as 1,800 volts were sent through the body. "There was the usual quivering of the muscles and the jump into the straps."[146] The current was kept on for a minute and then reduced. The body sank back, and doctors applied the stethoscope, searching for signs of life, but failed to find any.

REVEREND T.F. CARROLL, WHO had been Williams's spiritual advisor for several weeks, stated that the man had made a full confession and repented. He was ready to meet death and until Tuesday morning had shown no signs of breaking down. Carroll had been with Williams since 4:00 a.m., praying with him and ministering the last rites of the Catholic Church. Williams spent his last hours in prayer, reported the *Semi-Weekly Journal*, "but as the time drew near when he was to go to meet his death he became nervous to the point of hysteria. Of a degenerate mentality, the fear of the cornered and helpless animal overcame him." Yet his mental state did not include the amorality of an animal; he was "shaken with the fear of what the great beyond had in store."

Although his "rambling valedictory," in the words of the *Watertown Re-Union*, convinced most witnesses that he was mentally deficient, "Williams' crime was so outrageously brutal and fiendish that he is not an object of sympathy," noted the *Livingston Republican*. The equally unmoved *Democrat* noted Williams's death as the moment the current "put an end to his rambling" and supposed that he meant he was the aggressor in the fight when he said he was the one. Although Williams was spared the posthumous excoriations to which the press had subjected other executed criminals, the public was left to fill in the obvious blanks when assessing the perpetrator of a crime that the *Syracuse Journal* reminded them was "heartless and horrible."

Chapter 10

CHARLES SPRAGUE

Jerusalem, Yates County
1911

By 1911, the Idlewild hotel on Keuka Lake's Bluff Point, long past its prime, had transitioned into a private residence. In a nearby cottage dwelt the property's owner, eighty-two-year-old Pascal Van Lew, whose daughter, Minnie, and son-in-law, George Martin, had joined the household after the death of his wife that spring. He rented to Charles Sprague, who lived in the hotel with his wife and three children. Sprague worked the place on shares but took advantage of Van Lew's absence to help himself to whatever he wanted; when dividing the produce, he invariably took more than his due. Van Lew objected, "but rather than to have an out and out break with Sprague, let matters drift."[147]

George Martin, about thirty-four, was physically strong and reticent, declining to enter any argument with Sprague. His neighbors considered him "a most estimable citizen, attending strictly to his own affairs."[148]

Sprague was to dig potatoes as part of the agreement but ignored Van Lew's frequent suggestions to do so. Van Lew consulted a Penn Yan attorney, who, displaying the wisdom of Solomon, recommended Van Lew dig every other row. Van Lew complied with the lawyer's suggestion.

The morning of October 17, 1911, Sprague, who had allegedly been drinking at Keuka, returned and found the family harvesting their share of the crop. Flourishing a club, he told them, "Get off from this land."

"I guess I will not get off my own land," replied Van Lew. He began to pick up the potatoes, but Sprague grabbed the tray out of his hands and threw it into the ravine.

"I will get a gun and shoot you," Sprague threatened before storming off.

Minnie, alarmed, begged her father and husband to leave. Van Lew and Minnie went home around noon, but when it looked as if it were about to rain, George said he would bring in the rest of the crates. While Minnie prepared the noon meal, he went back to the field, reassuring her that Sprague was a coward and did not have a gun.

In the meantime, Sprague had walked nearly a mile to the home of his uncle, also named Charles Sprague, and procured a rifle. When the uncle asked Sprague what he was going to do with it, he said there was a pheasant he wanted to kill in the potato field.

The first knowledge Martin had of Sprague's presence was when he called out to him and said he was going to shoot. As Martin straightened from picking up the potatoes, Sprague, standing about fifty yards away, shot him in the abdomen. Martin collapsed and rolled down a ravine, whereupon Sprague came over and looked down at him. Martin closed his eyes and feigned unconsciousness, when he heard Sprague mutter, "---- you, if I thought you weren't dead I'd shoot you again." Martin did not dare move for some time, lest Sprague carry out his threat. Sprague evidently went back to his uncle's to return the rifle, and after about fifteen minutes, Martin made his way home.

Minnie had become anxious over George's long absence and was about to join her father in searching for him when he staggered in, covered with blood that ran from his wounds and holding his sides. "Charley Sprague shot me," he said. "Go after a doctor and an officer."

The nearest telephone was an eighth of a mile away. To reach it, Minnie would have to expose herself to Sprague's gunfire if he were in the vicinity, and she had reason to believe he would be. A bank screened her part of the way, and she reached the neighbor's, out of breath. She asked some men she encountered to go to the scene, but none dared, fearing that Sprague would shoot them.

While Minnie telephoned for help, Sprague's uncle answered and was told that his nephew had shot George Martin. He had Minnie hold the wire while he questioned his nephew about the accusation. Sprague admitted that he had shot Martin, adding, "Why, what about it?" His uncle told him if he had, he had better give himself up. Sprague then went to his own home, where he remained until a deputy sheriff and policeman came to arrest him. When asked why he committed the crime, Sprague replied that he and

The "X" shows where Minnie Martin stood when she heard Sprague make his threat. The Idlewild hotel is on the left, with the Van Lew/Martin home on the right. *From the* Penn Yan Democrat, *February 9, 1912.*

1. Path taken by Martin to reach home. 2. Door through which Martin entered house after being shot. *From the* Penn Yan Democrat, *February 9, 1912.*

Martin had been quarrelling all fall, that he had forbidden his digging the potatoes and that "he had made up his mind that he would be boss."[149]

A hole in the back of Martin's right side indicated that the bullet had gone through, and such a wound led to expectations of recovery. During the night, however, Martin gave indications that he was seriously injured, spitting up black blood and suffering great pain. He rapidly worsened the forenoon of October 18 but was able to relate the story of the shooting to a friend who came to visit. He died of his injuries at 1:30 p.m., ten minutes after he signed his statement, at the home of his brother-in-law.

The postmortem examination showed that the bullet entered about two inches below the breast bone, cut off the gall bladder, passed through the liver, severed a piece of rib, came out of his side and lodged in a bone near the right elbow.

"SPRAGUE'S APPARENT UNCONCERN IN the awful crime he has committed appears to show his nature," the *Yates County Chronicle* stated on October 25. "The feeling in the neighborhood ran high for a while as there seemed to be no kind word for Sprague, who is generally conceded to be a lazy, worthless bully, and apparently a degenerate. He had established a reputation of such character that he had been told to get out of one town and one farmer, to whom he was well known, said he would not have him on his place under any conditions." The *Chronicle* revealed that Sprague had once picked up a chair and threatened to strike Van Lew. "The latter, old as he is, backed up a step or two and then dared Sprague to make good on his threat."

Sprague was taken from the county jail to the justice of the peace court at Kinney's Corners on October 23 and was held for the December grand jury on the charge of murder in the first degree. Depositions were read to the prisoner, who remained emotionless at all times. His representative, attorney Abraham Gridley, asked for and was granted a private examination, allowing one witness at a time to be present and excluding all spectators and the press.

Abraham Gridley. *From the* Yates County Chronicle, *February 9, 1912.*

Minnie, who by chance was seated opposite Sprague, "fixed upon the prisoner a look so piercing that had he possessed any of the finer sensibilities he must have suffered. Try as strongly as she could, she was unable to keep her eyes from his face for more than a moment, and all the loathing and contempt that mortal could express without words shot from her eyes. The intensity of her gaze and the struggle for control of her feelings, made an occurrence that was dramatic in the extreme. Through it all Sprague sat apparently indifferent."[150]

Mrs. Sprague, said to be a hardworking woman who took in washing while her husband smoked on the front stoop, did not "appear to realize the seriousness of the trouble her husband has created, for she expected that he would be let out on bail during good behavior."[151]

ON DECEMBER 6, 1911, the grand jury returned an indictment against Sprague, charging him with murder in the first degree. As he had no funds to engage an attorney, Gridley was assigned as his counsel.

The trial opened on February 6, 1912, with William Clark presiding. In his brief opening statement, District Attorney Spencer Lincoln of Penn Yan announced that the defendant would forfeit his life if convicted of the crime, and the people would show, by Martin's dying declaration, what took place.

Minnie Martin testified to the events of October 17, with her father corroborating her story. He added his own narrative of an earlier altercation: "About the time grapes commenced to get ripe I spoke to Charley about pasturing his horse in the vineyard. Horse had eczema and rubbed up against everything and broke down the stakes. I told him to take a scythe and cut what grass he wanted and feed the horse outside the vineyard. He was going to break my head, pound in my face. He came after me with a chair. Martin saw him do it. Martin didn't do anything."

Top: William Clark. *Bottom*: Spencer Lincoln. *From the Yates County Chronicle, February 9, 1912.*

Martin had never said a word against Sprague, according to Van Lew, and had nothing to do with him. When asked if Martin said something about giving Sprague a licking when he came up to them in the potato patch, Van Lew claimed that Martin had said, "You have reported around you are going to lick me. Now is a good time to do it." Sprague did not offer to strike Martin and left about half an hour later to get the gun.

After a discussion of Martin's wounds, the people's case closed late in the afternoon. The defense moved that the indictment be dismissed and the defendant discharged on the ground that the prosecution failed to prove the charge as made in the indictment. The motion was denied.

One of Sprague's attorneys, James Sebring of Corning, claimed that the Van Lew family got together and decided to charge Sprague with premeditated murder and that the shooting was "purely accidental." They had deprived "this poor man and his wife and children" of fruits and other things, leaving them little or nothing. The thought of shooting anyone had never entered Sprague's mind; claims to the contrary were manufactured by the Van Lew family for the purpose of convicting him. The bullet in Martin's body had struck a hard substance that flattened it, causing it to glance and turn around completely before entering his flesh. The cartridges from the rifle, shot at a distance of fifteen rods, would have gone entirely through Martin's body.

Sprague was placed in the witness box at the beginning of the morning session on February 7 and was still answering questions by the noon recess. He said he would be thirty-three on his next birthday and had been born in Rushville, Yates County. He had an older sister and five younger siblings. His father was killed when he was twelve, and from that time he had resided in Sherman Hollow in the town of Jerusalem. At seventeen, he married Nellie Rector and thereafter lived mostly in Yates County, working on farms. About seven years earlier, he had been arrested for fighting with his father-in-law, the only other time a criminal charge had been made against him.

Sprague said that he had known Van Lew about twenty years, "during which time I have done more or less work for him." Until the spring of 1911, his relations with Van Lew and his daughter were friendly. He had known George Martin about three years. He outlined the terms established when he moved to Van Lew's property (e.g., he would plow the grapes, and Van Lew would allow half payment on the rent). Sprague said that he had planted his half of the potatoes and that Van Lew was to furnish the other half. When Van Lew gave him a picking box full, Sprague said they were not enough and asked for more. Minnie said there weren't any more, and

Sprague planted some he found on the hill. He did not think the potatoes were ripe and fit to dig by October 17—the tops were still green.

Sprague claimed that they'd had a "controversy" that summer over some fruits and pasturing a horse in the vineyard. "At this time I told him if he was a man of my age I would slap him, and he put his hand in his hip pocket and said, 'I will shoot you,' as if he was going to draw a gun."

In Sprague's version of the events preceding the shooting, he'd taken groceries home and started for the potato patch, bringing along a piece of buck-saw he'd found on the way; he supposed his children had been playing with it. Martin was picking up potatoes, and Sprague told him to get out of the patch, that he had no business there. "I did not take the land from him, and he had nothing to do with the potatoes." Martin came up to him and said he'd taken counsel, who told him to dig every other row. Van Lew said he could pick the rest if there was anything left. "Martin caught me by the shoulder, and I told him I wasn't there for trouble. Martin had his hand back to strike me, and I told him I did not want any trouble with him and turned and walked away. Van Lew called me a — —, and dirty thief, and said I stole from him all summer." Sprague denied ever threatening to shoot either of them.

He said that he went to his uncle's to borrow a potato digger, but when rain began to fall, he changed his mind and borrowed a rifle to go hunting, as he had seen some pheasants and squirrels on the way. He searched the woods for game without finding any and went to a peach orchard above the vineyard to look for rabbits. He saw Martin in the potato patch and hollered three or four times for him to get out. As Sprague walked along, the gun exploded, and Martin turned around and walked out of the patch. He did not fall or stagger and went behind the barn out of Sprague's sight.

Neither on direct nor cross-examination was Sprague asked to explain how he came to press the trigger. He was carrying his gun under one arm, he said, as hunters sometimes do. He claimed he didn't know he had shot Martin when his uncle questioned him about it.

Sprague answered the district attorney's questions without hesitation, according to the *Rochester Democrat and Chronicle*, and he "steadfastly clung" to his story. Several character witnesses were sworn on Sprague's behalf that afternoon, and although cross-examination of these "developed nothing of much movement against the defendant," "some things not entirely to his credit were testified to." Frank Collin, for example, could not say that Sprague's reputation was good; he did not please his employers and was supposedly of a "somewhat quarrelsome disposition."

1. Where the wheelbarrow stood. 2. Where Martin stood. 3. Where Martin fell. 4. The knoll on which Sprague stood. *From the* Penn Yan Democrat, *May 5, 1916.*

The *Democrat and Chronicle* pointed out that the month the shooting occurred was a closed season against killing pheasants and that these birds were seldom hunted with a rifle. It was maintained that a rifle was the only sort of firearm Sprague could obtain at the time, and the closed season was not respected as much by people living in the vicinity of the game as it was by residents of Albany.

Fred Plaisted and Ward Ellis testified to experiments they had performed with the rifle. Three shots went through ten three-quarter-inch boards at a distance of 250 feet. At 300 feet, a bullet went through five boards, a two-inch plank and eight inches of pork. The defense considered these tests of great importance and contended that if Sprague had directly fired at Martin, the bullet would not have stopped when it struck the arm bone but instead would have passed through.

After the defense rested, a number of witnesses testified to Sprague's bad reputation. Charles Scott, although he personally knew nothing against

Sprague, said that he'd heard he was a lazy, indolent person and did not work much. His neighbors thought he was a bad character and were afraid to cross him in any way. Van Lew denied ever threatening to shoot Sprague while he lived on the Idlewild property, and neither he nor Martin ever carried a firearm on the premises. Court adjourned for the day.

BOTH SEBRING AND LINCOLN presented their summations the morning of February 8. Sebring contended that the shooting was accidental and that if the jury accepted that defense, it must acquit the prisoner. Lincoln informed the jury that there was no middle course for them; the jury members must either find the prisoner innocent or convict him of murder in the first degree. Referring to the test of the powers of the rifle with which Sprague did the shooting, the district attorney ridiculed it "as being in no way evidence that a bullet would not be flattened in passing through a man's body and striking the forearm bone."[152]

Although the jury was out nearly four hours, only one ballot was taken, and the opinion that Sprague was guilty was unanimous. Sprague heard the verdict "without a tremor."[153] When Justice Clark asked Sprague if he had anything to say, Sprague replied that he had not had a fair trial, that there were people who should have been called on his behalf but were not. The court told Sprague that his defense had been "conducted ably by one of the best lawyers in Western New York" and that no fault could be found.[154]

Clark immediately sentenced Sprague to die in the electric chair the week of March 17. A motion for a new trial was denied. Sprague heard the date fixed for execution with the same outward composure as when the verdict was announced. His wife wept and clung to her children.

Gravestone of George Martin, Lakeview Cemetery, Penn Yan. *Photo by R. Marcin.*

THE MOTION FOR A new trial was denied again in May 1912, after Gridley appeared before Justice Clark and presented his appeal on the grounds that two jurors allegedly expressed the opinion that Sprague should not be given a trial but should be electrocuted without expense to the county. Clark ruled that even if they had made such statements, this did not disqualify them. Although it was conceded that witnesses testified to the jurors' comments, they were made during a time of excitement over the murder, in casual conversations with neighbors and long before they were summoned as jurors. When these jurors were examined as to their qualifications, their answers showed that they were "absolutely impartial" and could and would decide the case on evidence alone.

Gridley filed another appeal in August that acted as a stay of execution. It was claimed that Sprague was the only prisoner in Auburn convicted of murder, and the state maintained an electric plant in the city at a cost of $500 a month solely for him, as all future electrocutions would be in Sing Sing. The *Rushville Chronicle* reported that Sprague hoped the bill recently introduced to abolish capital punishment in New York State would save him from the electric chair.[155]

Three years elapsed before a motion for a new trial was scheduled to be presented on May 31, 1915. Gridley and Sebring were to argue for the defendant; Lincoln and District Attorney Charles Wood of Yates County would oppose the motion.

A number of Yates residents who were in Penn Yan at the time of the trial made affidavits stating that jurors had been permitted to mingle with the people and that they were influenced in their decision by popular clamor for Sprague's conviction. One allegedly said before being placed on the case that he would vote to convict Sprague if he were accepted as a juror. Clark declared that a careful reading of the moving papers and affidavits convinced him that "this application is without merit, that the defendant had a perfectly fair trial before an intelligent and impartial jury…and that the verdict was fully warranted and supported by the evidence."[156]

Lincoln made a motion before the Court of Appeals for a dismissal of the appeal because of the dilatoriness of Sprague's attorneys. The motion was denied. However, the Court of Appeals removed Sprague's attorneys on the grounds that they did not attend to the case properly, and Lewis Watkins, of Watkins, was appointed in their place.

Watkins, new to the case, took time to prepare, and in February 1916, he appealed Sprague's conviction and Clark's decision denying a new trial. In March, Justice Frederick Collins wrote the opinion that Sprague was guilty

Charles Sprague. *From the* Penn Yan
Democrat, *March 31, 1916.*

and that, providing the governor did not commute the sentence, Sprague must pay the death penalty the week beginning May 1. He would be the first Yates County murderer subjected to capital punishment, as well as the last person executed at Auburn prison.

A final effort to save Sprague was made the last week of April 1916, when attorneys Gridley, Amasa Parker and Calvin Huson made application to the governor for an order commuting his sentence. A petition signed by many Yates County residents, procured by Sprague's mother, asked for executive clemency, to no avail.

Sprague was visited by a sister and other relatives on Saturday, April 29, and on Sunday his mother was admitted to the death cell. She was "led away sobbing bitterly, but the man did not break down," according to the *Auburn Advertiser-Journal.* His wife did not come to the prison.

Sprague had never gone to church and professed no religion, but on Sunday, the night before his execution, he decided to embrace faith. The chaplain administered the sacraments of baptism and communion, after which Sprague prayed for some time. Upon Sprague's request, the warden sent him a chicken dinner and "many other good things."[157] The prisoner ate well and slept some during the night.

Five minutes before he was led into the execution room on Monday, May 1, Sprague wrote in a steady hand on the fly leaf of the chaplain's Bible, "I have got to leave this world, but I wish that I could leave it knowing that there would not be another drop of liquor sold." He had told the chaplain that he blamed liquor for the trouble he was in, although to the last he denied the murder, insisting that Martin was killed accidentally. Sprague was resigned at all times, the chaplain said, and did not once break down, although until twelve hours before his death he entertained the hope that the governor would commute his sentence to life imprisonment.

Sprague's mother and aunt were with him before he exited his cell at 5:30 a.m. The chaplain recited prayers as he led the march into the death chamber, but Sprague did not respond. He waved one arm slightly toward the witnesses and said, "Good morning, gentlemen." His last words, delivered clearly, were "I am innocent." After he was seated, he looked steadfastly at the witnesses, showing no trace of fear.

The voltage was "the customary death dealing application," but Sprague was a large man, nearly six feet tall and about 220 pounds, and "his resistance to the current was fairly powerful."[158] The straps confining him creaked as his body shot forward.

After one minute, the current was switched off, and the doctors made a careful examination. The heart was still beating faintly. After the second shock, which lasted five seconds, Sprague was pronounced dead. It had been eight minutes since the prisoner had entered the room. The *Advertiser-Journal* proclaimed the execution "in all respects successful, no hitch of any kind occurring."

The body was removed for the customary autopsy, and that evening, undertakers brought the remains to Penn Yan. A private funeral service was held at the Friend Church, with interment at Friend Cemetery.

NOTES

Chapter 1

1. *Geneva Advertiser*, November 13, 1894.
2. *New York American*, May 1, 1829.
3. *Geneva Daily Times*, May 28, 1929.
4. *Geneva Gazette*, April 22, 1829.
5. *Geneva Gazette*, June 3, 1829.
6. *Seneca County News*, November 20, 1888.
7. *Geneva Gazette*, June 3, 1829.
8. Ibid.
9. Ibid.
10. *New York Spectator*, June 1829.
11. *Geneva Daily Times*, September 11, 1888.
12. *Geneva Advertiser*, September 11, 1888.
13. Ibid.
14. *Geneva Advertiser*, November 20, 1894.
15. Ibid.
16. *Geneva Daily Times*, September 11, 1888.
17. Ibid.

Chapter 2

18. *Auburn Weekly American*, February 13, 1856.
19. *Auburn Weekly American*, February 6, 1856.
20. *Auburn Daily American*, August 31, 1855.
21. *Auburn Weekly American*, September 5, 1855.
22. *Auburn Daily Advertiser*, March 28, 1856.
23. *Auburn Daily American*, February 16, 1856.
24. *Auburn Daily American*, February 2, 1856.
25. Ibid.
26. *Auburn Daily American*, February 4, 1856.
27. *Auburn Weekly American*, February 13, 1856.
28. *Auburn Daily Advertiser*, March 28, 1856.
29. Ibid.
30. Ibid.
31. Ibid.
32. Ibid.
33. Ibid.
34. Ibid.
35. *Penn Yan Democrat*, April 2, 1856.
36. *Auburn Daily Advertiser*, March 28, 1856.
37. Ibid.
38. *Auburn Weekly American*, April 2, 1856.
39. *Auburn Daily Advertiser*, March 28, 1856.
40. *Auburn Weekly American*, March 28, 1856.
41. Ibid.
42. Ibid.
43. Ibid.
44. Ibid.

Chapter 3

45. *Wayne Democratic Press*, February 8, 1860.
46. Ibid.
47. *Wayne Democrat Press*, November 2, 1859.
48. *Finger Lakes Times*, October 21, 2012.
49. *Syracuse Daily Courier*, March 26, 1860.
50. *Rochester Union*, March 24, 1860.

51. *New York Herald*, April 3, 1860.
52. Ibid.
53. *Geneva Times*, March 27, 1962.
54. *New York Herald*, April 3, 1860.
55. *Syracuse Daily Journal*, February 1, 1861.

Chapter 4

56. *Geneva Gazette*, December 2, 1870.
57. *Geneva Gazette*, June 24, 1870.
58. Ibid.
59. *Geneva Gazette*, December 2, 1870.
60. Ibid.
61. Ibid.
62. Ibid.
63. Ibid.
64. Ibid.
65. Ibid.
66. Ibid.

Chapter 5

67. *Auburn Daily Bulletin*, October 17, 1872.
68. *Auburn Daily Bulletin*, October 15, 1872.
69. *Troy Daily Times*, October 10, 1871.
70. *Auburn Daily Bulletin*, October 16, 1872.
71. Ibid.
72. *Auburn Daily Bulletin*, October 22, 1872.
73. Ibid.
74. Ibid.
75. Ibid.
76. *Evening Auburnian*, September 6, 1879.

Chapter 6

77. *Evening Auburnian*, July 23, 1880.

78. *National Police Gazette*, August 7, 1880.

79. *Buffalo Courier*, September 3, 1873.

80. *Auburn Weekly News and Democrat*, October 10, 1873.

81. *Evening Auburnian*, July 22, 1880.

82. Ibid.

83. *Evening Auburnian*, July 23, 1880.

84. Ibid.

85. Ibid.

86. Ibid.

87. *Evening Auburnian*, July 24, 1880.

88. *Geneva Gazette*, July 30, 1880.

89. *Evening Auburnian*, July 24, 1880.

90. *Evening Auburnian*, July 31, 1880.

91. Ibid.

92. Ibid.

93. *Weedsport Cayuga Chief*, August 7, 1880.

94. *Syracuse Standard*, August 11, 1880.

Chapter 7

95. *Ithaca Daily Journal*, March 17, 1888.

96. Ibid.

97. Ibid.

98. *Trumansburg Free Press*, March 17, 1888.

99. *Ithaca Daily Journal*, March 20, 1888.

100. Ibid.

101. *Ithaca Daily Journal*, October 18, 1888.

102. *Ithaca Daily Journal*, October 25, 1888.

103. Ibid.

104. Ibid.

105. *Ithaca Daily Journal*, October 26, 1888.

106. Find A Grave, www.findagrave.com.

107. *Ithaca Daily Journal*, October 10, 1889.

108. *Ithaca Daily Journal*, March 28, 1890.

109. *Auburn Advertiser*, in *Ithaca Journal*, March 28, 1890.

110. *Ithaca Daily Journal*, December 28, 1892.

111. *Ithaca Daily Journal*, August 13, 1895.

Chapter 8

112. *Watkins Review*, December 25, 1907.
113. *Watkins Review*, April 10, 1907.
114. Ibid.
115. *Elmira Free Press*, April 4, 1907.
116. *Watkins Review*, April 10, 1907.
117. *Elmira Star-Gazette*, December 11, 1907.
118. *Elmira Star-Gazette*, December 18, 1907.
119. *Watkins Review*, December 25, 1907.
120. *Elmira Star-Gazette*, December 20, 1907.
121. Ibid.
122. Ibid.
123. *Elmira Star-Gazette*, February 27, 1908.

Chapter 9

124. *Avon News*, February 22, 1911.
125. Ibid.
126. *Syracuse Journal*, February 22, 1911.
127. Ibid.
128. *Livingston Democrat*, June 7, 1911.
129. Ibid.
130. *Livingston Republican*, June 8, 1911.
131. *Livingston Democrat*, June 7, 1911.
132. *Livingston Democrat*, June 8, 1911.
133. *Livingston Republican*, June 8, 1911.
134. Ibid.
135. *Syracuse Journal*, June 3, 1911.
136. *Rochester Democrat and Chronicle*, June 3, 1911.
137. Ibid.
138. *Livingston Republican*, June 8, 1911.
139. Ibid.
140. Ibid.
141. *Livingston Democrat*, June 7, 1911.
142. *Auburn Citizen*, June 5, 1911.
143. *Livingston Republican*, June 8, 1911.
144. *Auburn Semi-Weekly Journal*, August 2, 1912.

145. *Syracuse Post Standard*, September 12, 1912.
146. *Auburn Semi-Weekly Journal*, September 17, 1912.

Chapter 10

147. *Yates County Chronicle*, October 25, 1911.
148. Ibid.
149. *Penn Yan Express*, October 25, 1911.
150. *Yates County Chronicle*, October 25, 1911.
151. Ibid.
152. *Rochester Democrat and Chronicle*, February 9, 1912.
153. Ibid.
154. Ibid.
155. *Rushville Chronicle*, February 27, 1914.
156. *Penn Yan Democrat*, June 11, 1915.
157. *Auburn Advertiser-Journal*, in *Penn Yan Democrat*, May 5, 1916.
158. Ibid.

BIBLIOGRAPHY

Arcadian Weekly Gazette.
Auburn Advertiser.
Auburn Advertiser-Journal.
Auburn Citizen.
Auburn Daily Advertiser.
Auburn Daily American.
Auburn Daily Bulletin.
Auburn Semi-Weekly Journal.
Auburn Weekly American.
Auburn Weekly News and Democrat.
Avon News.
Buffalo Courier.
Cayuga County Independent.
Elmira Free Press.
Elmira Star-Gazette.
Evening Auburnian.
Finger Lakes Times.
Geneva Advertiser.
Geneva Daily Times.
Geneva Gazette.
Geneva Times.
Ithaca Daily Journal.
Ithaca Journal
Livingston Democrat.
Livingston Republican.

Lyons Republican.
National Police Gazette.
New York American.
New York Herald.
New York Spectator.
Oswego Palladium.
Ovid Gazette.
Penn Yan Democrat.
Penn Yan Express.
Rochester Democrat and Chronicle.
Rochester Union.
Rushville Chronicle.
Seneca County News.
Syracuse Daily Courier.
Syracuse Daily Journal.
Syracuse Journal.
Syracuse Post-Standard.
Syracuse Standard.
Troy Daily Times.
Trumansburg Free Press.
Watertown Re-Union.
Watkins Review.
Wayne Democrat Press.
Weedsport Cayuga Chief.
Yates County Chronicle.

ABOUT THE AUTHOR

R. Marcin, a resident of the Finger Lakes region, has contributed historical features to the *Watkins Review & Express* and the *Observer*. She studied languages at Elmira College and has a master's degree in French literature from the State University of New York at Binghamton. This is her first book.